Close to Home

Close to Home

✦

A Soldier's Guide to Returning from War

Britta Reque-Dragicevic

iUniverse, Inc.
New York   Bloomington

Close to Home

A Soldier's Guide to Returning from War

Copyright © 2008 by Britta Reque-Dragicevic

iUniverse books may be ordered through booksellers or by contacting:

iUniverse
1663 Liberty Drive
Bloomington, IN 47403
www.iuniverse.com
1-800-Authors (1-800-288-4677)

ISBN: 978-0-595-48901-5 (pbk)
ISBN: 978-0-595-50906-5(cloth)
ISBN: 978-0-595-60888-1 (ebk)

Printed in the United States of America

"*Close to Home: A Soldier's Guide to Returning from War* is a beautifully written, courageous, and inspiring guide to surviving the difficult and often agonizing return home from war. One of the most important books to be published since 9/11. It is a life saver, compassionate, well-researched and timely. It should be required reading for every American."

—Ron Kovic, Vietnam veteran, author, *Born on the Fourth of July*

"This is an important book because it confronts an issue which thousands of soldiers face—how to return to "normal" life after war ... and adjust to families who often have become more independent and assertive in their absence. For those who fought, coming home means leaving behind probably the most important and intense experience of a lifetime, and often finding no one who really understands, and many people who don't really care. Britta Reque-Dragicevic's well-written book offers thoughtful suggestions to returning soldiers on how to find new meaning in life and to rebuild relationships; and to their friends and loved ones on how to deal with the men and women returning from the battlefields in Iraq and Afghanistan."

—Edith M. Lederer, co-author of *War Torn: Stories of War from the Women Reporters who Covered Vietnam*

"Britta's book is a very strong and courageous effort to deal with a subject that's almost impossible for anyone to grasp if they haven't had war experience in some form, which even then eludes us. It contains a great many thoughtful ideas, including some not generally addressed, about the difficulty of coming to grips with war's after-effects on the individual and on relationships."

—Richard Pyle, former Associated Press Saigon bureau chief

"*Close to Home* is a how-to-guide that brings together the experience of "being there" with survival.... War has no favorites; we are all affected whether it is the soldier, family, or friend. By sharing her experiences, Britta has fueled my belief that together we can make a difference—one person at a time."

—CPT Patricia Curry, U.S. Army, Iraq

"You are obviously a special individual who *gets it*."
—SGT Mike Pectol, Vietnam veteran and PTSD survivor

Acknowledgments

There comes a moment in life, a shimmer of insight, when you know that you were born to do exactly what you are doing. This book is one of those moments for me. It is born out of love and created out of soul. I believe that we are all connected and what affects one, affects us all. I also believe that the Universe leads us to the sources we need. If you are reading this book, it is because it is meant to come into your life. This book has a purpose in your journey.

While soul-purpose is ultimately up to each of us to fulfill, no book is ever born from a single soul.

This book is no exception. From my friend who came home from Iraq and stood before me unmasked, to my sister who is now heading toward her second tour of war, to my father who died a veteran who had never been heard—their souls and their stories are woven in to the spirit of this book.

Life would not have chosen me to write this had it not been for my loving husband, Alexandar (Sasha) Dragicevic, my dear mother-in-law, Rada Drljic, and my Associated Press family in Sarajevo: Aida, Amna, Sava, Degi, Eldar, Amer; Zdravko, and the many, many Bosnians who showed me how survivors live after war—with vulnerability and resilience and beauty and friendship.

I don't know if I would have had the courage to complete this book if it were not for the unfailing compassion and encouragement of Remy Benoit,

Paula Griffin, CPT Patty Curry, SGT Jeff Anderson, Edith Lederer, Richard Pyle, the work of Drs. Ed Tick and Kate Dahlstedt and the support of my Vietnam veteran friends: Ron Kovic, Sgt. Mikie, Harry Kieninger, Lonnie Story, John Cory, Terry Bell, Michael Broas, Michael Kuehlewind, and of the many others who read drafts of this work and gave comments, insight and courageous feedback. To all of you I say: thank you.

This book is part of us all.

Lastly, I want to thank my amazing children, Gregor and Sara, who through my giving birth to them, gave birth to me, and light up my soul every moment. I love you.

Contents

Foreward

What is war after all, but a classic love story? Boy meets gun, boy falls in love with gun; boy and gun live unhappily ever after.

The Ville by John Cory[1]

I was given this gift of darkness, wrapped up in red, white, and blue with sparklers for ribbon. It was a curse, still is at times, but often enough it has become a favorite gift, like a hideous necktie given on some special holiday; ugly, at first, but eventually placed among the favorites for its unique color and design.

When Britta asked if I would include something in this book, I immediately said yes, and then backed off with second thoughts, wondering what I would have to contribute to her valuable and most necessary project. All I can offer to her beautiful work is a journey, incomplete and ongoing, the destination unclear and unimportant, just a fellow traveler who may or may not be up ahead or somewhere behind you. This is our road, no matter where it leads: there are hands to hold in the darkness; whispers to be heard from those who have passed; and knowledge posted on signposts from our kindred spirits who journey with and all around us.

Dear Brother and Sister Vet:

There are ghosts of war, and not just the frightening ghosts of the dead or maimed, but cheerful friendly ghosts that fill me with a strange comfort and longing that "normal" people never will comprehend. And I like that. This is mine.

I turned nineteen in the Vietnam war and then twenty, the Senior Aidman (Medic) for my infantry unit. I was "Doc," the parish priest to whom guys turned to confide and confess their sins and fears, to everything from needing a shot of penicillin to ward off a dose of the clap to wanting a friendly ear to lament the latest "Dear John" letter, or the letter from friends and family members that some "Jody" was making time with their girlfriend or wife. Sometimes it was just an evening talk where nothing was really said, and yet the fear of the future and the present were wrapped in phrases like "don't mean nothin,'" or "there it is" or my favorite, "what are they going to do to me—send me to Nam?" Every word danced around the real topic— the war—and pointed directly or indirectly to "the World," that alien bright planet whirling out in space somewhere. The place we were from, but couldn't remember, and the place we dreamed of going if only we could.

Our native tongue became the language of war; and we became fluent in it, this shorthand of anesthetic adjectives and verbs that wrapped us in body armor for the soul so we could deal with it all. We could "light 'em up" or "grease 'em" or "kill them all and let God sort them out," or "Fuck 'em! It don't mean nothin'..." The dialects of the language of war change from generation to generation, but the basic language remains the same.

I don't know what I expected when I rotated out. The way it worked in those days never really dawned on me until years later, when I began to study the reasons for my insanity and failure to fit in. The devastating and maniacal brilliance of how they made my war work was truly cold and calculated and completely disorienting.

We were plucked one at a time from all over the place, packed into an airplane and processed on arrival. Strangers with the only connection being we were on our way to the Big Green. Once there we were sorted, and sent out to spend the next thirteen months or eighteen months with our units. There we would wage war, and bond with an intensity of friendship and camaraderie like no other. Blood, sweat, and tears, and then, the short-timer calendar checked off, we would hop in the Huey and be lumped together for out-processing and dropped back on the block in the dead of night, arising the next morning in the old neighborhood with all the old friends and relatives ready for us to get on with life. One day, smelly fatigues and some asshole trying to blow you away, and two nights later back home—as though you'd never left.

The morning after my return, the old woman who had raised me gave me her list of chores. "Jack's been ill so you need to mow the lawn. It's looking ragged and I don't want the neighbors to think we're lazy. That nice Williams girl was asking when you were coming home. You could do worse, but her parents are the kind of people we like and it wouldn't hurt to say hello. I talked with Donna about you getting a job with the VA, and she said you should stop by this week for an interview and fill out the forms. You won't have any trouble getting a job with them, and you can start within the week. Your cousin, Dick, gave me the university enrollment package and the GI Bill forms and said you need to get those going now so you'll have the money when school starts next month. And Ross Turner wants you to stop by now you're back. He was always asking about you—we never mentioned your refusing to carry a weapon. I don't think any of us could understand that, and your brother said it wasn't really patriotic, even with your medals. No need to embarrass anyone."

And there it was. From Senior Medic and veteran to lawnmower, student, and hospital orderly in less than seventy-two hours.

Two weeks later, I was at my girlfriend's sorority party. A stranger in a strange land who could not 'grok.' The girls chatted about dates, bridal showers, upcoming engagements and the latest on who would marry whom and when. The guys talked about their 'major,' not my kind of 'Major'. These were pre-law, business, pre-med majors—stuff of the future built on their last two years. Everyone talked about movies and television shows I had never heard of, the latest fad sweeping the campus, and cars, and going into the family business, and all the things they had been doing here in The World, while I had been in The Nam.

My world had been life and death and these guys were bitching about putting a ski trip together and conflicting schedules and finals and whatever. And they were nice, clean-cut college boys who didn't appreciate my occasional "Fuck it, man! It don't mean nothin' just go for it," or my great evening faux pas, "Man I'd like a little short-time boom-boom with that chick." This having been said to the guy she was engaged to, unbeknownst to *moi*!

And inevitably came the questions when they found out I had not been at college, but at war. My answers were polite and stilted, screened carefully while my brain raged on and on at the lot of them—the whole stupid gaggle of them:

> *Them*: Wow, the war huh? What was it like?
> *My Brain*: What the fuck you think it was like?
> *My Mouth*: Crazy people shooting and trying to stay alive.
> *Them*: You kill anybody?

My Brain: No, but I could make an exception with you.

My Mouth: Don't know.

Them: Were you at My Lai? You know, with Lt. Calley?

My Brain: Yeah, I was, and I want to do the same thing to this stupid-ass party right now!

My Mouth: No.

Chick Them: I think you guys should work for peace now that you're back.

My Brain: I'd like to work for a little piece of you, baby!

My Mouth: What's your name?

And there were the nights. Quiet. Empty streets. Everything shut down while people rested for the coming morning school, and work, and all that other stuff. But not me. I went for drives, cruising the streets in the bad part of town, looking for a bar that would sell me a drink even if I wasn't twenty-one yet, and maybe fill up the quiet with a jukebox and the clatter of a pool table. For months I made friends with hookers who, for a price, would tell me lies about how special I was and how I deserved some loving after doing time in 'Nam. And in the daytime I was acceptable to society, working at the hospital, trying to overcome boredom in classrooms, and listening to my girlfriend and her family lay out the new life we were going to have.

Schizophrenic to the max! Nothing made sense. I was a thousand pieces of a jigsaw puzzle, but all the pieces were either olive drab in color or sky blue, so no matter how hard I tried to make them fit, there were no markers or borders or landmarks to use to make sense of the puzzle—just thousands of tiles that had no rhyme or reason or shape.

People all around me acted like I was crazy or just wild, and needed something normal to settle me down and make me focus on "real" life and school and job and marriage and the future. But I was living the future I had dreamed about while I struggled to survive the world I had known before my inter-planetary travels had landed me here.

I caroused and cruised every dark corner I could find. Spent nights at the VFW club listening to the 'real' Vets from WWII tell me what a 'real' war was and what it took to be a man in a 'real' war. And for the price of a round or two, they'd even let me throw in a couple of combat tales, let me confess to them all my warrior sins and civilian failures, and then we'd drown our sorrows together. Even drunk and belligerent, they were Vets and I could talk to them—carefully and guarded. They didn't want to hear about some crazy-ass medic who threw away his rifle and refused to ever carry it again because he thought the war was wrong. Didn't care that he did his duty because he believed it was his duty to serve his country—just not to kill others who were fighting for their country. No room for middle ground. The enemy was the enemy and a solider had to kill the enemy, or else there would be no victory. And every war had to have a victory. That was a rule.

But my war didn't. And that was the shame. There were no more 'good' wars.

I was jealous of school chums who had gone on with their lives, some of whom hadn't even known that I'd been to war, while others seemed to ignore my combat experience as irrelevant to the world of jobs and school and achievement. They were on their way to Yale and Harvard and I should have been on my way to Brown University instead of wasting two years fighting a stupid war, for what? For what reason? Man, the questions we ask ourselves about war can drive us nuts.

And then one day out of the blue, Gordy called. Just passing through and wanted to get together for old-time's sake. It had been six months since we had left Nam. Just a quick get together. *On my way, brother. On my way.*

It was a two-day bender. Still can't tell you where all we went and what we did. Drunk for two days swapping lies and memories about the tour, laughing at the stupid shit we did or got caught in, and the somber moments requiring double shots when certain names and days came up, and the bad death and the good death. "Least he didn't suffer, blown to smithereens in one big boom. Not like Lake who took that round to the head. Heard from his sister that he's a vegetable over at the Nashville VA. Fucking-A. I want to go out clean and done. No lingering bullshit, no limbs missing. Just dead. Plain gone dead, man."

The more stories we recalled or invented for one another, the more we re-lived the war and that old axiom, "How do you tell the difference between a war story and a fairy-tale? A fairy-tale starts out 'Once upon a time...' and a war story starts with 'This ain't no shit...'" And the truth is, our memories were caught in a limbo of being home while trying to find that touchstone of war that once made us part of some greater whole and at the same time relieved us of the guilt for not being there with our brothers, even now. All we wanted was to remember—and forget—all at the same time.

Winding our way through the streets of life and war, we were trying to escape and evade the police. Being the clever survivalist-based veterans that we were, and me knowing the lay of the land, we hung a sharp right off Highland Drive and straight onto 13th East and then another swerving maneuver across a grassy hillside, gaining speed and out of control, suddenly launched airborne, we found ourselves coming in for a hard landing in the middle of the pond at Sugarhouse Park, engine running uselessly, water pouring in over the low-slung doors of the canary yellow '57 TR4, five squad cars with bubble-gum lights flashing and cops rolling on the lawn in laughter while others glared at us across folded arms.

Gordy took a long pull on the bottle of Old Grand Dad and passed it over to me for a swig, a wistful smile at our captors. "What are they gonna do Doc, send us to 'Nam? Don't mean 'nothin."

A few months later during a late night of drinking my brain cells away, I called Gordy. It was 3:00 AM, the normal calling hours for drunks looking for lost love or old friends. His phone had been disconnected. I never saw or heard from Gordy again. Just like the war, we were there and then we were gone.

Over the next few years, I would seek adventure and release via the wild and unruly actions of all lost boys. I called it fun, while others called it drunken obnoxiousness and irresponsible behavior. Didn't matter, it had to be done; I was searching for release from a prison I had no idea I was even in. Nor did I understand that the "fun" was a cover for anger and grieving that had never been completed.

There were days and nights when I would pull out photos and little pieces of memorabilia just to touch them again as though their touch would put everything right, make me whole, or let me sleep in peace. When that failed, the unexplained rage inside me boiled up until I tore up photos, threw the medals and citations into a box and sealed them away never to be looked at again. I destroyed a lot of what was so very important to me in those days and only a few pieces remain today: a few brown Polaroid snapshots in a scrapbook; a tattered fragment of cloth; and the worn boxes of medals that my son discovered and wanted to know more about just a few years ago.

I can't tell you the date of the first time that I talked to my ghosts. It was years and years after I had left the war. It was one of those nights where depression and insanity all ganged up on me and filled me with an eternity of sadness that felt like it was smothering my very core. It was one of those nights when you know the world is going to come to end and take you with it.

People have no idea how hard it is to work at keeping "sane" or "normal" when the chaos inside of you is demanding to be let loose in order to wreak havoc on the unsuspecting world around you. Or how that chaos offers you salvation even at the peril of your own destruction and how very comforting that can feel. Suicide is salvation, just a millimeter away.

It all started out on a day as normal as any other. I worked long hours, came home to get kids delivered according to football practice and school activity schedules and all that normal stuff, then later in the evening, pulled out moving boxes to sort through what was important and what could be discarded. And there it was: a cardboard box full of ghosts—photos, certificates, medals and the letter.

A short time after the war I had written a letter to Pat Lambooy's parents. I wanted to visit his grave at Arlington and then stop by to meet them and pay my respects. His mother had written back giving me directions to his grave, but declined to meet with me. It was, she said, "…too painful a reminder of their loss and to look at someone who had survived only served to intensify the anguish of Pat's death and the capricious nature of war."

The wave of guilt and sadness and rejection slammed into me with a fresh intensity that brought it all back. I had survived. Pat was dead. And the way he died that September day came back in violent Technicolor.

Vin Loc. Rainy. The only high ground to pitch camp above the flooded rice paddies was a cemetery. War is full of irony, and to keep dry and get some rest meant we would become neighbors of the dead.

I watched the first RPG launch from the left tree line and sail overhead, splashing down in the rice paddy behind us, without exploding. I watched two VC weave in and out of the trees and open fire with AK's, followed by three others with more RPG's—more accurate, and this time, deadly.

Chaos and noise. "Medic! Medic!" Gunfire while everyone scrambled for cover. "Medic! Medic!" I ran to the shouts, ducked for cover while a few rounds sprayed the mud and headstone rock into my eyes. I was on autopilot. Follow the screams and locate the bodies. One leg wound, not bad, just chunks of lower thigh chewed open. Pressure bandage, morphine, and 'hold on' encouragement while I moved on to the next, and the next. The one that concerned me most was the body lying just outside our perimeter in the open. Had to get there. No movement, but he could still be alive.

I splashed out through the sludge and water, grabbing the body and pulling it to me, looking for the wounds. Just the one. The RPG had hit him in the helmet and part of his head was open, gray matter hanging out. The guy was gurgling, not going to make it, but damned if I'd give up on him. More splashes as guys gave me covering fire and arrived to help me carry him over to the staging area for the Dustoff bird to get him back to the hospital fast.

Bandaged, telling him, "Hang on! Just hang on and we'll have you out of here in no time."

The Medevac swooped in and we loaded the wounded. I passed on the medical tag info to the door-gunner and crew and off they went, swallowed by the gray clouds and rain.

The firefight was over.

Time to double check on everyone, take a breather and do the usual sit-around with Doc Daniels and Pat and Doc Jo-Jo. Talk it out fast so it didn't hang around and cloud our minds before the next one hit. Walk it off. Talk it off.

I couldn't find Pat. Doc Daniels asked if I wanted to sit down with him. No. Where's Pat? Jo-Jo tried to talk with me, but I couldn't hear him, just watched his mouth moving—the sound drowned by wind and rain. Where's Pat?

Daiwi (Captain) Fivian grabbed my arm and pulled me aside before I could go any further. In that wonderful, warm, calm manner that endeared him to his men, he stood in front of me—making sure my back was to the men so they wouldn't see the impact—and with his one hand gripping my shirt, as much in comfort as control, he said, "Doc, you put him on the Bird. He's gone." His eyes held me firmly in place letting the truth settle in.

My brain screamed at him: "No! I didn't! No! He's around here someplace, I just can't find him! I know who I put on the bird and he wasn't one of them!" But Captain Fivian's eyes never left me. The truth was there, and the truth rattled my teeth and chilled my bones.

My best friend. The one guy I had come to know so well and share so much with was dead. Half his head gone. My friend. I hadn't recognized my friend. I was so robotic in gathering and treating wounded men that I never recognized my best friend. Never saw his face, only the wound. Leg wound, head wound, shoulder wound, or sucking chest wound—all the same. Categories for treatment and triage. Never people—not until long after everything calmed down. Even my best friend. How fucking numb can you get in war?

Yes, years later there was the survivor's guilt, but the gift that kept on giving was the failure to recognize. Death was a part of war, just plain fact. Failing to recognize the dead, just plain sin. Why would his family want to see me? Meet me? They probably knew how cold and dead I had become, so who could blame them for not wanting to look at me?

And there I was, nearly fifteen years after the war reliving my sins from a cardboard box and the rejection of others unwilling to revisit their own pain and loss. I started to weep and then hours later and long after midnight, I was still bawling like a baby and blubbering and shaking and sputtering to catch my breath. It would last for more than a month, overwhelming sadness and heartache, more than a decade of yesterdays suddenly so alive and fresh that I could taste the rain of that day, and smell the damp wood and rice paddy water. And it wouldn't go away.

One afternoon I took off from work and life and everything around me. Suicide offered an end, but little comfort—why would it? I was crazy, that's all there was to it. Couldn't get over a silly frigging war and one death. What the hell was wrong with me? Everything. I was wandering around the dark caves inside of me, trapped and caught in the crossfire of reverberating echoes of pain and guilt and everything bad about me and my life. No future, no real feelings to offer anyone: inflicting misery and insanity on everything and everyone I loved—if indeed I did love. Maybe I couldn't love—how depressing is that? A walking, talking piece of stone. What was the point of going on?

I began to talk to Pat. Not out loud, at least, not at first. *Why didn't you let me know who you were? Grab me and say my name? Why did you have to be outside the perimeter? Didn't I tell you every day that you had to stay close? You don't wander around trying to be the nice guy? Not in a place like Vin Loc. What the hell was wrong with you?*

Somewhere along the line, my mental ramblings became vocal, and people walked carefully around me, avoiding me, pitying me, and pulling their children away from me. "Watch out for the crazy guy on the pier screaming at the ocean."

By sunset, I had screamed and ranted at a roll call of the dead. Huffman, who I had to listen to as he died across the radio one night in October; Jo-Jo, who was there one minute and gone the next when a mortar round took him out; Smitty in June; and Eldridge, who had pushed me back to the middle of the platoon as we searched a village telling me, "Doc, you stay here, not on point, so in case something happens you can take care of the guys. No bullshit, no point leads, stick by the RTO." A few minutes later he would be screaming for me, both his legs blown off by a waiting booby-trap in the bamboo thicket I had just been searching.

They were all there as clear as could be, alive, and forever trapped in the youth that had killed them. But the living showed up too, like a black and white still life, the moment frozen forever: Poole, and his big Indiana grin when he found peaches and pound cake in his C-Rats; Winkler, jabbering non-stop about life in Minnesota; and Racine, ready for his career in semi-pro baseball. Elders doing the Dap while Archie Bell and The Drells played in the background, his big happy smile lit up the day every time the AFN played Motown hits over the radio. *Daiwi* James Fivian, a real officer and gentleman, who gave each man in the company his due and was as unflappable as any man I had ever known when the shit hit the fan. He was as masculine as bourbon straight up, and ever mindful and caring of his men. There was Captain Tucker in his homemade Santa suit, .45 on his hip and white mop-head yarn for his hair and beard when he jumped off the Bird to deliver care packages for everyone a week before Christmas. And Captain McMahon from Tra Bong, the ever-present half–chewed, half–smoked cigar and his words of wisdom when I ran out into the middle of a mortar attack to get the wounded helicopter crew and found myself in the midst of exploding rounds and whizzing bullets—completely alone. He said, "Good job, Doc. But next time you yell, 'Let's go!' you might check to see if anyone heard you."

Funny thing is, they gave me peace. Not a lasting peace—that was still years away—but for the time, for that day and a long time afterward, I found reason to be angry and reason to grieve, even though I didn't know that at the time, or understand what I was going through. After years and years, I had found the need to talk about the war, the people, my friends, and my brothers. And God help the person who just asked one of those innocent questions like, "Janice said you were a Vietnam vet?" because the floodgates had been lifted and I would trap them in a corner and try to tell them all about the war—in one sitting. People avoid you when you do things like that. You scare the hell out of them. Asking you about the war, to them, is just like asking about the weather or how you're doing—they don't really mean for you to answer because they aren't really that interested. Someone forgot to tell me that part.

Over the years that followed, I bored people to death; innocent citizens became collateral damage to my dumping a whole rice paddy in their laps at one sitting. Poor bastards. And the old drinking crowd suddenly joined AA or became Unitarians or some other damn thing just so they wouldn't have to listen to me, and the process of sorting fiction and fact that had encased my memories. From sullen silence to warp speed jabbering in twenty-five words or less. It wasn't that I was obsessed, but even counseling groups reformed and changed meeting schedules to avoid me.

One day I was telling a couple of war stories to a friend, who happened to be a psychologist, and she said, "You should write that down. Write a story or a book." And it began.

The Gulf War/Desert Storm was just kicking off, and the whole country was rallying behind the troops—people were writing songs, movie stars were lining up with care packages and USO shows, and the politicians were scrambling to make speeches of support and promised legislation that would atone for the sins of Vietnam and all the 'disrespect' given a previous generation of veterans. I got pissed.

Where the hell were all of you before? Where were the veteran programs now being promised for the past twenty years? Everybody was there to write movies and speeches and whatever, to make a buck. Where had they been when we needed them? When I was crazy and needed some outlet? Some safe harbor of release? Where the fuck were all of you then? It don't mean nothin' now!

So I wrote a story. Vietnam Vet father faces his daughter entering the service and going to war, Desert Storm, and after a few months of instant combat and surrender, she gets parades and welcome home parties all over the place while he is a passing note at the bottom of the newspaper article, 'SSgt. Casey Long was one of the first female helicopter technicians to serve in actual combat support roles. Her father, also a veteran of a different war, is justifiably proud of her service to her country....'"

My anger came back with a vengeance. Writing the story had been a therapeutic experience, but it touched a nerve and that opened everything else that had been dammed up for so very long. I was back reliving the bad old days and talking to ghosts. But this time, the ghosts talked back—and that scared the hell out of me.

It wasn't voices in my head, or the usual self-talk we all walk around with; for me, it was oh-so-very-real and so very good because they talked back. It would take a few more years for the conversations to settle into something I could deal with, but my God, it was a two-way street, and I wasn't insane anymore. Maybe a little crazy, but not insane.

One day I was passing an art gallery in San Francisco down by Pier 39 and was struck by the pieces on display. I couldn't take my eyes off them and so I went inside to find out something about the artist. Modern pieces, squares and patches of various colors and hints of primal shapes while others were frenetic lines of energized chaotic colors ripping and slashing across the canvas. I found out they were expensive because lots of folks were equally fascinated and captivated by the artwork. I couldn't afford them, but I met the artist—an older guy (my age) who discovered his talent in therapy for PTSD. Go figure. We went down to the Eagle Café and spent the morning over coffee and conversation, looking for salvation and finding yesterday and common tattered threads of our war in Nam and the war at home and the war inside us. We even had our own body count of casualties: two ex-wives, failed businesses, family that no longer spoke to us, shrinks we'd driven to seek their own counseling, and a road map of failed relationships and 'almost made it' relationships.

It seems the peace we are taught we need, never comes. "The war" is never over, and, in my opinion, should never be expected to be "over."

One afternoon, Jack M. called me to his office, just to talk. Jack is part of Tom Brokaw's "Greatest Generation" although he would tell you all that is just a bunch of hooey! Each generation is different and great in their time for their own reasons. Jack was my landlord, owner of the small shopping mall where I had opened a retail business soon to be doomed, but he and I had shared several talks previously, so this afternoon wasn't unexpected. Ah, the beauty of the unexpected.

Jack opened a bottle of his private stock—you know, the good stuff. Poured a glass for me and one for him and ever so slowly wove his way through business talk, the need for the downtown association to step up and help shopkeepers, and all those mundane necessities we use to gently frame what we really want to talk about. Eventually the talk turned to a group of black and white photos on his office wall. "You recognize anybody up there?"

I went for the obvious choice of trying to pick the young version of the man who sat across from me. It took a bit of time, but I zeroed in on young Jack—and then the guy standing next to him. Pencil-thin moustache, fashionable in those days, slightly over-large ears, cap cocked to the side, and big grin. It was Clark Gable. Movie star. Regular Joe—bombardier pilot— part of the squadron when young Jack at the tender age of twenty became a bomber pilot based in London.

Impressive.

And then Jack held his own roll call, pointing at curly haired all-American boys one by one and gave me the thumbnail sketch of their lives; hometown, future plans, made it out or 'bought it' over Dresden or Stuttgart or Hamburg. Killed by Ak-Ak or *Messerschmitt* or dumped in the drink after flying as far as possible on damaged engines. For some he laughed, for others, he talked quietly, and for a select few he openly wept small tears and in hoarse voice, whispered "God rest their souls. I remember them as though it was yesterday. And you understand that, which is why I needed you to sit with me this afternoon."

Fifty years, brother and sister vet, fifty years. Jack shared his ghosts of war with me and still knew each and every one of them. And so we spent the afternoon talking, as men often do, of the shared experience—and the knowledge that our language was that of a brotherhood born in pain and the desire for redemption without ever forgetting.

So what's the point to all my ramblings?

The point is that I love you, dear brother and sister vet, as much as I can love anyone in this life. And yes, we are crazy—not insane—but a little crazy, because the human soul was never intended to endure the violence, loss, alienation, and pain of that terrible sweet beauty that is war.

They say that the first casualty of war is truth, but they are wrong. The first casualty of war—is reality. In war, the unreal becomes real, and the truth is a lie.

—*The Ville*[2]

I have no answers for you, only a shared journey. For some the journey is long, and for others, it comes quickly, but is unending, as it should be.

We were warriors once, and still. There is a unique beauty to our very core and our very survival. And we need to embrace that wonderful part of ourselves that survived the mayhem and chaos and utter devastation called war.

The day we are not traumatized by the monstrosity of war, we allow "them" to switch on the meat grinder and run even more honorable men and women through the political hamburger machine—and they will then be abandoned and discarded like rusted toy soldiers left in the rain.

Now I've told you everything I "don't know," and you have the right to ask, "What *do* you know?"

Brother and Sister Vet, this is what I do know:

I know parades are nice, but not necessary. The parade of fellow vets extending a helping hand is worth more than all the applause in the world.

I know that if the Greatest Generation can still feel the pain and power of brotherhood, and still know the names of the dead and living, half a century later, then survival is worth the trip in order to sustain the traditions and respect and honor that comes with being a veteran.

I know this book by Britta is a good thing.

I know that our families become collateral damage in our own struggle to deal with our war. And I know that somehow, without expecting them to ever understand, we have to work at understanding all the things they have carried in the empty days they lived while we did battle.

I know that I can tell a good war story to others, and only the truth to another vet.

I know that it is okay to be a bit crazy, because that keeps us from going insane.

I know that I don't see dead people, I just talk with them—even when sober. And that's a good thing.

I know that if you ask, I'll listen, and if you never ask—I'll still be there for you.

I know that the jumble of a thousand pieces can make a whole jigsaw puzzle picture if it is given enough time and the tools to do it—no matter how skewed up and lop-sided it turns out to be. I may look like a Salvador Dali painting on the outside, but on the inside, I'm still apple pie, Mom, and America, with a red, white, and blue twist.

I know 'one klick' equals one thousand meters of eternity. I know that you hump 5 klicks in and never come out. That the map that says 'You are here" is lying. Like the old Firesign Theater line: "How can you be two places at once when you're really nowhere at all?"

I know that battlefield injuries are only skin deep, while the heart is wounded forever.

I know that you are precious and honorable, that you are my brother and sister veteran and that we will never forget—and that will heal us one with another.

Not long after my return from Vietnam, Ross Turner invited me over to his basement one day. The basement where, as a boy, I had strapped on his canvas leggings and field pack to run and play soldier with the other boys in the vacant field at the end of the street.

Ross was a Guadalcanal Marine.

"Don't tell your old lady I gave you this beer," he said. "Just wanted you to know that we're all proud of you and what you did over there—and what you stood for. Don't let anyone ever tell you different."

It took a long time to remember his words and to understand what he was telling me.

The next time I talk with Pat and Huffman and the others, I'll let them know that you are out here now trying to put it all together. They know the road, and they'll walk point for you.

—John Cory, Vietnam veteran

Prologue

Jake pulled into the schoolyard. I heard his truck door slam, and glanced up as he sauntered over.

I hadn't seen him since he'd returned from Iraq. "Hey, how's it going?" I asked. We stood next to my SUV, watching our kids scamper across the playground. Jake's son was six— mine was four—both blond and blue-eyed—reflections of our Scandinavian heritage.

"Good. What're you up to these days?"

"Writing, full time. I just finished a novel." I leaned on the open back passenger door; my two-year-old daughter sat in her car seat, nibbling a cookie, eyeing us carefully.

"What's it about?"

"An American forensic scientist in Bosnia. She discovers the remains of two children who died hugging each other, and becomes obsessed with finding their truth."

Jake squinted in the afternoon sun and nodded. He'd served in Bosnia while I'd been living there.

"I wrote it for Bosnians actually, to remind them that despite their scars and everything they've been through, their souls are still beautiful."

Jake's sun-lined face fell silent. I wondered if he knew that his soul was still beautiful.

We watched our kids for a moment.

"So, how is it being back?"

"It's tough." Jake shifted his weight and stared off as his son climbed to the top of the slide.

"You know, if I could just get some sleep—I get three, four hours a night—if I'm lucky," he glanced at the pavement, then back at me.

"Nightmares."

I nodded. He didn't have to say more.

"It's just really hard for me to relate to people," he whispered.

"It'll take time."

"Yeah. A lot of time." He grinned half-way, took a breath and the fatigue poured out. Did he believe in time? He wore a positive attitude like a Boy Scout badge. It matched the smile on his lips. It didn't match what I saw in his eyes.

Jake's son ran up and hugged his dad's legs, his eyes lighting up as he chatted away. Jake smiled and took the heavy backpack from his son's small shoulders.

"We'll see ya," Jake said as they headed toward their truck.

Sadness sank into my chest.

He wasn't anywhere close to home.

I'd seen him six months earlier when he'd been home from Iraq on leave, and still had been himself; fun-loving, laughing, spirited, able to interact as if we hadn't seen each other since prom. Now he was an old, old man. My age, thirty-one.

I drove home sobered by the realization that what I had just seen is what happens when we keep soldiers on the battlefield too long. That there is a line we cross—a day, a point in time, one second even—when a soldier kills one too many insurgents, lives through one too many near-deaths, watches one too many buddies get their faces blown off. And is asked—no, ordered—to stay one day, just one day, too long.

Back at my house, I sat at the computer. Somewhere between being home on leave and coming home for good, Jake had crossed that line. His National Guard unit had been fighting in Iraq for a year and a half. His unit was scheduled to return to Minnesota in March. Much to the outrage of their families, their mission had been extended until July, a twenty-two month-long combat mission—at that point, the longest deployment of any military unit in Iraq. Jake had arrived home early due to a family emergency.

An email popped up on my inbox; I shut off the screen, uninterested in my day's writing. The image of Jake, of what my soul recognized in him, threw me off center. It raised emotions I had dealt with and held back for years. The ravages of war. The price the soul pays. The unending questions that strip your nerves raw.

Jake and I were nine when we met. He grew up to be tough, loyal, strong, humorous, a well-loved platoon sergeant. The kind of guy who works twelve-hour days at his family business, volunteers at community clean-up; and teaches his son to fish. Not the well-muscled man who'd stood next to me dangling from life's edge. My strongest memory of Jake was playing 'army' as kids—me a bit of a tomboy and he an all-out military enthusiast—we'd line up bucket loads of little German and American army men in mounds of beach sand until the Americans fought and won Normandy. Then we'd line them up, fight, and win it again the next day, and the day after that. We were addicted to old *Combat!* re-runs and John Wayne World War II flicks. As teenagers, Jake collected antique military gear, and I fell in love with people who were dying in the Balkans. Jake joined the National Guard and at twenty-four, I headed to Sarajevo, married a Bosnian war survivor who was an Associated Press war correspondent—and lived and reported from a society that felt war's wounds deeply. I knew that haunted look. I knew what it felt like to have the ravages of war steal your soul. I'd almost lost mine.

I returned to America when we were at the height of our own war. Time, distance, a new baby—it took more than two years just to begin to feel that wholeness could be possible. To rise above the murky waters of incredible suffering which my husband, family, colleagues, and every single person I had met in Bosnia had endured, to find solid ground to climb up on and catch my breath. To rest. And wait. And rest. And watch as life continued to breathe through me, in and out, until, slowly, I regained consciousness.

I woke to realize that what I had been through in a post-war society, the questions I had lived, were ones my generation and our parents were just beginning to ask. Questions that war presents, but does not answer. True, the Iraq war was not mine—not in the emotional sense that Bosnia had been. I don't know Iraq intimately like I know the streets of Sarajevo, or to avoid landmines in Bosnia's hills. The conflict there in Europe ended over a decade ago. For many, it's long forgotten, 'old news.' But what war does to the soul is not.

War transcends time, space, place, societies. It bridges cultures, race, religion—it is, perhaps, one of the most fundamental experiences that unites humanity. Survivors, veterans, anyone who has had war touch their lives knows its mark, can trace the scar tissue over its incision, can feel the instant bond when eyes meet: "You were there, you know a part of me that no one else, but the two of us, can know."

As my husband, Sasha, likes to say: "You had to be there, to know."

I haven't been to war or lived through it. I'm not a survivor. So how can I write this book, you ask? And why should you read it? It's true, I'm not a psychologist, and I don't have a PhD behind my name. What I offer you is my experience as a human being whose life journey has taken me into depths few civilians have ventured—life in a post-war zone. I've lived in the aftermath of war, in the devastation that haunts a country and survivors for a lifetime. I live with and love a survivor. For years, I listened carefully and compassionately to survivors talk about their war experiences and faced their pain with them. I learned to discern when to gently ask questions and when silence and a hug were most needed. I learned that listening and non-judgment are often the greatest contributors to healing, and that the act of sharing pain can break the isolation emotional trauma so often induces. As a journalist, I wrote about the remains of war until my heart bled, fought back tears recounting one too many mass graves, and learned the intricacies and surprisingly resilient nuances that human beings develop in response to war. I know survivors. I know the dead. I know fate's shadow, the thin, thin line we walk on, and the abyss on each side.

And I know what war has done to my soul.

The emotional and soul wounds that war inflicts are universal, but finding your way to a healing journey is not. Many are searching for this path. I have been blessed to have had enough personal exposure to the devastation of war to have had my own soul forever altered, and then to have been given the grace to find a measure of healing—or, perhaps, better put, a new sense of wholeness. I am very humbled to have the honor of offering you what I have learned, and, in some sense, to walk with you on your journey.

This book isn't meant to replace the wisdom and training of healthcare practitioners—although I hope that it will find its way as a companion to such care. I truly respect and cherish the work of licensed practitioners, and I know that they offer healing guidance and answers that truly make a difference. Sometimes, though, it helps to read advice from those who aren't "experts" and, more often than not, in my own journey, it has been "regular people" who have appeared in my life to offer the guidance I needed. They shared their humanity with me, had the courage to offer their own opinions, and freely gave the gifts of insight and guidance that the Universe had taught them. That's what this book is all about. It is simply a personal conversation with you, born out of deep love and care for those who have survived war, and those who love them.

Strangely enough, I hadn't planned to write this book. I didn't think I had the right to say anything. But when I saw Jake and his son, I knew I had to. I had to share what I had learned, and the path to renewed meaning that I had found. I had to stand up and say something. Not just for war survivors, but for their children. For the next generation who will now grow up affected by war's ocean-spanning tentacles. For the children who have endured countless nights crying for daddy or mommy, facing a child's ultimate fear—that mommy or daddy will never come back. Of course, they don't understand everything that's happening, but they know their parents are brave people who fight for freedom. They know that, everyone tells them that, but all they really want is for mommy or daddy to come home. To be okay again.

That's why our hardest battle is yet to be fought. The battle to find wholeness, to not feel shattered into a million little pieces, to someday believe in good again. We have to reach down inside ourselves, and know, beyond a doubt, regardless of the darkness we've created or endured, that underneath it all—our souls are beautiful.

Because your soul is still beautiful.

And your life has just begun.

As you read this book, know that you are held close in the Universe's loving embrace—that there is unlimited grace, abundance, and compassion for you. You may not feel it now, but that doesn't change it. It's there.

This book is designed to be read in short spans. Many war survivors find they have shortened attention spans, and sometimes have difficulty reading and processing information at length. Feel free to jump in, read a few paragraphs, skip around. Revisit the pages that have meaning to you. If something seems irrelevant, or you disagree, skip it. If you never finish, that's fine, too. This book is *for you*. To say what you may not be able to say. To help you give yourself the words for what you are experiencing, what you may want to share with others, and some straightforward advice and suggestions for dealing with it. It's also for caring family, friends, and healthcare practitioners who want insight into what life after war is like—and real-life advice for how to approach it and how to help.

You'll find at the end of each chapter a section called "Voices"—where veterans have shared their stories and experiences with you. Following each chapter, there are two blank pages, called "What's Running Through My Mind Now"—use those to write down your thoughts, make notes or give voice to what you are holding inside. You can also access more information and resources at this book's website, http://www.lifeafterwar.org.

Hold on to your vision and your hope. You are not alone.

For wholeness,
Britta Reque-Dragicevic

1

Expectations

◆

"I'm fucking tired of looking at war! First it was our war, then Kosovo, and now anytime something bloody happens, we have to be there!" Eldar said. He set his heavy Associated Press TV camera down on the floor, took off his cap, plopped down on a swivel chair, and rubbed his aching shoulder. My husband, Sasha, walked in after him, and sat down. He and Eldar, along with Amer, our TV producer; Degi and Sava, our two photographers; and our driver, Eso, had just returned from covering a landmine explosion. Two children had been killed.

"It never stops," Sasha said, shaking his head and downing a Coke. Their ashen faces and hollow eyes betrayed what they had just witnessed. The war had been over for more than five years, but people still died by landmines. I knew what I saw in my colleagues' eyes was not the horror of fresh death; but the fresh flashback of three years of having escaped death surrounded by blood pools and body parts.

I stirred the frothy pot of Bosnian coffee and poured the coffee into espresso cups. The head of our office, Aida, and I had written the short news story and sent it to the editing office in Vienna.

She took off her glasses and rubbed her eyes. She'd cried as we'd gathered the facts about the two children whose bodies had been ripped in half.

"I'm tired of this, too. But what else can we do? This is all we know," Aida said.

The room fell silent.

War was all they knew, *now*. It was hard to remember what had come before. Aida had been a German translator who could write in English— during the war, she'd been separated from her toddler, balancing her son's safety with her own chance for survival. AP had hired her early on to work in their war-time office. Eldar was a cinematographer. A five-hundred pound rocket had sent shrapnel slicing into him; he'd survived the attack and continued covering the war. Amer had been a college kid studying English when he'd landed a job as a producer for APTV. He'd been eighteen when a grenade killed his mom. Degi had been a war prisoner and dodged death; Sava had taken innumerable risks to capture poignant images the world didn't want to see; and Eso had honed survival skills that had saved our crew more than once.

Sasha had been a journalist before the war. As an editor and on-the-ground reporter for Bosnian State news, he'd plowed through every day of Sarajevo's 1992–95 siege while heading up a crew of journalists. He'd dodged snipers, mortars, and starvation. AP snatched him up toward the end of the conflict that had pitched the country's three ethnic groups—Serbs, Croats and Muslims—against each other in a bitter battle for independence from Yugoslavia.

They were survivors. Some might call them victims, but "survivors" is a more accurate term.

Aida went back to her desk to take a call. Eldar left for the day to pick up his son at school. Sasha and I sat at the table, coffee gone.

"How did I get this life?" he muttered, shaking his head. Beads of sweat still traced his hairline. His cell phone rang.

"Vienna?" I asked, having followed his side of the English conversation.

"They want more details."

How did I get this life? My husband wondered. It wasn't what he—or any of them—had expected.

War ends. Fighting stops. People stop being soldiers and start being moms and dads and teachers and mechanics and computer analysts again, right? Your spouse welcomes you with open arms, your kids hug you, your boss seems pleased that you're back. Life is supposed to move on. You're supposed to put the war behind you. Get on with things. Forget about it.

No. War ends. Fighting stops. One day you're killing insurgents, the next you're sitting at home wondering if you'll ever get rid of images of severed heads and the charred bodies of kids with birds picking out their guts. Your spouse seems uncomfortable around you. Your kids are thrilled to see you, but you don't recognize them after a year or more away. Since you've been gone, your employees have slacked off. Finances are worrying you, and yet, how the fuck can money matter now? You're supposed to feel lucky, right? After all, you survived. You made it home. You did your duty. You thought the whole country was behind you. Now it looks like life here at home went on pretty much the same as if the war had never happened. In fact, no one seems to pay much attention to the war at all. And your buddies are still back there getting shot at. People keep asking you how you are. You say it's tough. Some listen, most don't really want to know. You learn to say you're fine.

This isn't what you expected. How did you get this life?

Life after war is not what we expect. *Life after war doesn't return to what it was before.*

I had no idea how pervasive war was until I'd lived in Bosnia for a few months. Nothing had been left untouched. From the currency in my wallet to not walking on mined grass to analyzing which stories we'd cover each day—the war remained in everything. It saturated me with every account of mothers having had their sons executed, children being uncovered in mass graves, and the constant ache I felt for the people around me. How could they live with such pain? As the years wore on, the pain crept over me until I couldn't see anything else. I felt my soul slipping away as I lost grip on everything that had once been my identity. The things I had firmly believed about life, God, goodness, the meaning of suffering slipped off like burning flesh. They were, simply, gone. My instinct was to try to hold on to remnants of self, to retrieve the lost parts of me. But what I didn't know then was that there is no going back.

After war touches your life, you can never be the same. War isn't an event, it's an experience. You may or may not feel this right away. And, depending on your role and personal experience, your reactions may not be as intense as others'. But don't try to convince yourself that you managed to escape your tour without it affecting who you are. It's simply not possible.

Families find this hard to accept. You want your loved one to be the same; to be okay; to not be changed. But assuming that he or she is the same is a mistake. When I fell in love with Sasha, I knew there were places in him I could never go—parts of him I would never understand. I could love him as he was now, the man I knew. In fact, loving him meant I accepted that there were parts of him created by the war. It wasn't my place to change or heal that.

What we expect of ourselves after war—and what we expect of our loved ones—is never the same as what really is. I had arrived in Bosnia full of compassion, Christian ideals, wanting to put my arms around a whole country, hold them close until their pain disappeared. I assumed I was stronger than war. I wasn't.

Instead, I was immersed in a city that could not see beyond the horror that still kept people silent on trams, eyes locked on the floor, afraid of looking up to see someone they had hurt or who had hurt them. People were in shock, unable to believe what they'd been through; how they'd destroyed their best friend's grandmother's house; locked up former classmates in freight-car torture cells and were powerless to stop snipers from playing cat-and-mouse as citizens weaved their way through alleys, doorways, and behind cars at night to fill a few gallons of drinking water.

I listened. I lived with and worked with people from all sides. Everyone was in incredible pain; most were in denial, steeped in grief and numbness. Stories abounded; tears freely flowed; the people I knew discussed the war. They reminisced, only to fall silent when it came to the hardest parts. The parts words would make too real.

I soaked it all in.

You may hate the person war has chiseled you into—heart beating with rage, anger, bitter, cynical, tense, over-emotional, empty, blank, cold, a lit fuse ready to go off at the lightest sound, touch, memory. Someone who knows too much. Or you may be dismayed because you seem to be just fine, and you're not sure if that's okay.

Life after war mires you into a complicated web of relationships, self-identity issues; and questions about healing. Your entire world—everything you believed to be true and real and solid—is shattered. You're left to try to recognize the pieces and figure out a way to put them together. All the while, you're expected to look, act and relate—normally.

Oh, Just Get Over It!

"John just isn't himself. I knew Iraq would be hard—what he's been through and everything, but I had no idea it would be this hard," Michelle said.

"What did you think it would be like?"

"I guess I thought he would have nightmares and stuff, but I didn't expect him to be so— different. He's like a ghost. It's like he's not here at all."

"Maybe he's not."

"What do you mean?"

"I mean maybe he's still in Iraq."

Michelle looked confused and shook her head.

"I don't know. Maybe he is. But the man living in my house isn't the man I married."

Michelle didn't know that I'd seen John back at his job at the bank.

"How's it going?" I'd asked. John looked at me, a blank expression on his face. He'd let stubble grow in.

"Not very good," he said quietly, glancing around. His eyes settled on my hands. "Michelle thinks everything should be back to normal. But I just can't get stuff out of my head. She just doesn't understand." He surveyed the bank lobby again. I followed his gaze. "I don't know. Everyone thinks I should just "get over it"—they tell me it's going to take time, but then they act like I should be as interested in their golf game as they are. Golf! All I can think about is what's going on over there. The guys I left behind."

Contrary to our society's beliefs, returning soldiers do not just jump back into the swing of things. When they try—and most of them do because bills have to be paid—they end up shoving their own needs aside, and settling into a routine that may no longer fit.

Guard troops, in particular, go back to jobs they had before, living out routines that keep them physically moving, filling in time during the day, but do not give them the place they need to heal. By going back to work immediately, survivors may be able to convince those around them that they are more okay than they really are. Wounds get ignored; the pain is masked better; everything you are feeling or not feeling gets shoved under the rug as you "role-play" the life you had. While this offers some comfort, in the end, it only puts off healing.

America has never been good at dealing with pain, death, or trauma. We prefer to pretend it doesn't exist, and expect our veterans to simply pick up life at home where they left off. A little welcome home celebration, a few rounds of drinks and an occasional 'How you doing?'—and we think we've supported our troops. Veterans are left for the most part to themselves, alone with their devastating experience and pain. Instead of having support systems where returning troops would have months to rest and heal, most are expected to be back at their jobs or reassigned duties within days.

As a survivor, you may have these same expectations. Going home is often equated with going back to the life you left behind. After all, you want so much for things to be as you've imagined. Images of making love with your partner, and seeing children smile and remembering how good it feels to chat with a friend is what got you through months of separation. Distanced, you fell more in love with your spouse; in your dreams he or she became more attractive, the little things that used to bug the heck out of you no longer mattered. The only goal you had over there was to survive another day and another night, to get home, to get back to that lover, to rekindle and express the deep love and passion that's built up and kept you going.

Then you arrive home to realize that while your partner is crying tears of joy to have you back, there seems to be an unsettling gap between you. You e-mailed; talked on the phone; wrote letters; sent and received packages; but the glaring reality sets in: life went on. Your partner at home is, amazingly, okay. Beautiful, strong, exhausted, but okay. Your kids have grown and have a new way of talking, new friends, new attitudes. Do they still need you? After two weeks of having you back, it doesn't matter much that you were gone at war. Since you're home, their lives are fine. But yours isn't.

You can't sleep. You have nightmares. Your body is still poised to fight. You see ghosts and the faces of those you've killed. You thought peace and quiet would be good, but now it's too quiet. Something must be up. Then you remember that you're in your backyard, and not Fallujah.

The person you were is missing.

What you know for sure is that you're not going to 'get over it' anytime soon. Realize and grab onto the fact that who you are now, after war, is *normal*. It's normal to feel dead inside, to not feel anything, to think and tell everyone you're fine; or to be angry, full of rage; and terrified. It's normal to be scared that you're never going to get your life back. It's normal to be worried that your partner is going to lose patience and leave you for someone else who 'has it together.' Or that your kids will be disappointed. Or that you may never be okay again.

Stop, take a deep breath and consider this:

You have been through some of the most devastating circumstances that a human being can experience. Realize what strength it took to endure this. It took an inner, tenacious resiliency to crawl through every day, every mission, every hell-filled night; and survive.

Underneath the rage and powerlessness and fear is a quivering spirit that has held on to life with all its might. It has held on to your courage, your hope, your innate compassion. It has held on when you believed it was over. It has held on as you washed the flesh and dried blood of your buddies off your trembling hands. It has held on and not given up and it's not going to give up on you now.

This core is your survivorship. It has allowed your body, your mind, and soul to do whatever they had to do *to get you through*. If that means that your soul has up and left, and your body is strung-out, and your mind cannot focus, that's okay. *Because you are still here.* You may not know why or even be happy that you are, but you are still here.

There's a reason for it.

Too Tired? What? Come on, You're Fine!

Whether or not you were physically wounded in battle, *you are wounded.* Deeply. And your wounds are real. It may take some time for you to become aware of it. In fact, war wounds are often buried deep inside. That's where that inner sense of being shattered comes from. That's why the fear exists that you're not really quite as okay as everyone thinks you are.

You expect to live normally in peaceful conditions at home, while your soul and body are still enmeshed in war. Your system has adapted to spending time in combat and survivor mode. It feels almost normal to you now, if for no other reason than that's what your body has been used to. Remember, though, that war—despite our system's amazing ability to adapt and become conditioned to it—is *not* a normal state of being.

In Bosnia, I spent my days putting victims, and survivors, excruciating stories into English words. I grew accustomed to writing about atrocities, body counts, groups of fathers, sons, and husbands shoved alive off five-hundred foot ravines. I became so familiar with the existence of genocide, concentration camps, and mass rapes that the words rolled lifeless off my tongue.

Along with my blindness to the fact that the situation I was living in was not "normal," came a deep fatigue. I wrote it off as culture shock and just kept moving forward. Without a second thought, I expected my body, mind, and soul to perform perfectly and lost sight of the fact that being wounded— emotionally and spiritually—under such circumstances was normal. What my body and spirit needed was compassion and understanding, recognition that I was *appropriately* hurting. Not a rap on the head and a "What's wrong with you?" crack.

Your body is no longer a machine or a weapon. Take a moment and think about that.

Your body *is* you. Your cells constantly reflect every stress and emotion within. Your body, mind, and spirit have embedded wounds. You are depleted. Your muscles have soaked up more stress than they can carry; your nervous system rails from extreme overdrive, pumping adrenaline and cortisol through inflamed arteries; your skin has taken a beating; your eyes are worn out; acid has eaten away your guts; your cells have suffered from lack of true nutrition; your lungs have been cramped, your ears damaged. And, if you have been physically wounded, you have added pain and suffering.

Imagine a child you love having been through what you've been through. Would you expect that child to simply arrive home after months in such conditions, change clothes, take a bath, sleep for a couple of days, and go back to school? No. Would you expect this child to never cry, break down, or show sadness? No. You would know that your child needs rest, deep rest, and you would not expect him to simply 'get on with it.' You would know deep within that your child needs everything possible—every ounce of nurturing and love and tenderness and compassion— to have the best chance to heal from such a horrific ordeal. You would make sure your child has the best food, rest, medicine, a soft place to sleep, and the freedom to cry in your arms.

You are somebody's child. And you deserve just as much compassion, from others and from yourself. Give yourself permission to be gentle with your body. Lower your expectations and demands. Don't berate yourself if you find simple things drain you. Your body needs time to recover, and it may take years before you are physically restored, or adapt to permanent wounds.

Don't expect your body to act as if everything is fine just because you're home. The damage has been done. This goes for your sex life, too. It's normal to not have the drive you once did or to experience dysfunction. It's also normal to be on sexual overdrive. The point is that we need to recognize that our bodies need time, gentleness, rest, and the chance to adjust without the expectation that it will happen fast.

Loving partners and families need to realize this, too. Even though a survivor may seem fine, war stress has impacted his or her body. Understand that it is going to take a long time to physically recover or adapt. We know war survivors endure trauma, and so we tend to focus on the psychological impact. We forget that this stress is carried, literally, in the body. Wounds to the spirit also manifest in the body, so it's not just injury or physical exhaustion that we're dealing with. If your loved one says he doesn't have the energy for something, believe him. *He doesn't have the energy.* The body needs nutrition, rest, massage, exercise, sexual release, and affection. It needs to be deeply and tenderly nurtured.

What Do You Mean: You Don't Know Who You Are?

Re-defining who you are after war can seem like an elusive process. We don't know where to look, or who to turn to for answers. Pieces are missing, beliefs have shifted. Survivors often simply feel broken inside. Confused. Uncertain. Alone.

You can be sure, though, that the core essence of who you are—the deepest parts of your spirit—are still buried underneath. Those parts of you will resurface when they feel safe enough to do so. They may be hiding to survive. Tender, loving, compassionate emotions, belief in good, in humanity, in life having meaning; the ability to trust, to have faith of any sort, the ability to feel connected—to others, to nature, to aspects of ourselves that we once counted on—all of this hides in order to allow the parts of ourselves that know how to survive death and violence to take over.

This is a gut-wrenching fact to deal with because we often desperately want to be the person we were before. We *liked* who we were—loving partners, affectionate parents, faith-filled church-goers, people who felt connected to Spirit, nature, our work, our purpose, the future, what we wanted in life. When we look at ourselves and feel disconnected—it's devastating. And yet, when we strip it down, everything we *believed* we were, is not who we actually are. Beliefs can change, and we still exist. It may take us a while to discover that we have the power to choose our beliefs, once we become conscious of them.

When we don't know how to define ourselves or what we believe, though, it scares us. It also scares our families. We have the comfort of knowing how we got this way. They don't. They sent you off with tears and paralyzed hearts and the next time they saw you, they were again embracing you with tears and hearts bursting with relief. You are to them, in every sense, the same person as when they last saw you. Except, you're not. What you know inside about how you feel, they can only guess at: watching you, looking for 'signs,' hoping beyond hope that you are okay.

Your family can't see inside you. Thank god, you say. But, hold on, that's not necessarily good. They can't see inside you, and that means they have no clue as to what you are going through. They have no reference point for the realities of war. Spouses are especially left in the dark. Most of us define a personal, close relationship with *how well we know another*. When there's this gaping hole in shared experience in our lives together, coupled with the fact that life has simply changed as time has passed, we feel alienated; and misunderstandings are inevitable. It's similar to giving two actors different scripts without telling them—they come on stage thinking they are both working from the same one. The result? Confusion and misunderstanding. You are working from your war script; your spouse is working from the script you had together before the war. Don't blame each other. You are simply living from the only place you each know how—your last reference point.

When we don't feel as if we really know someone anymore, we can start to worry about whether or not the relationship will survive. It takes a ton of commitment to make an intimate relationship work after war. One partner may feel this more heavily than the other does. As a survivor, you may be in too much pain to be objective enough to see how your pain is impacting the relationship. Spouses may worry they're no longer desirable or have the values and goals in common that first pulled you together and kept the relationship alive. You both start to wonder if this can still work. Fear sets in. Words get slung.

Stop. Take a breath. The essence of who you are is still within you. The person you fell in love with is still there. Changed, yes, but still there. You both need time to find out if your relationship can endure despite the changes. Remember, you have *both* changed, grown, and endured intense fear and stress.

What begins now is a journey to *become*, not to recover. To find out who you both will be. Hold on—and don't let go too early. This is not the time to give up on a relationship that is in its essence loving, supportive, and nurturing. (It is time to make sure you are safe, however, and if you feel physically threatened, you need to get help immediately.) Assuming that you're safe, though, you're going to have to find a way to be as mutually supportive of the relationship as possible. If that means you sleep in separate beds (or separate houses) in order to show genuine affection and acceptance during the time you are together, then do it. Do whatever it takes. But don't give up. Not yet.

So, Why Don't You Want to Pray Anymore?

Religion is one of the major issues war challenges and often changes. Loving families grow alarmed when a survivor returns and doesn't want to attend services, or no longer prays. It's especially hard if the family has held on to their faith as a key source of their strength.

Families need to realize that a survivor has had every tenant of faith challenged every single day by the act of killing, the breath of death, and the blatant suffering of children and civilians. What he or she experienced was much worse, and far more damaging, than you will ever know. It's hard for families to understand that what may be their source of spiritual strength may be a survivor's deepest source of confusion and anger. This is the reality for thousands.

I was a very religious person prior to living in Bosnia. One day in Sarajevo, as I sat in a new church listening to a visiting American pastor preach about not being afraid, and tell the congregation, quite sincerely, that God didn't want them to be afraid of public speaking anymore, I lost it. *How about being afraid your neighbor is going to rape you again? Or that you won't have enough food for tomorrow?* Real concerns of people in the room. I soon began to believe that the comforts of American Christianity simply do not deal with the realities of war.

War survivors need acceptance, not pressure, preaching, or convincing. If your loved one doesn't seem interested in religion, do not press her. She will eventually find her own spiritual path and, for many, conventional religion may never be part of their lives again. Don't let your own spiritual convictions prevent you from giving your survivor the open acceptance she or he needs right now.

Families may also experience the opposite. A survivor may have 'found religion' on the battlefield and, all of a sudden, your secular family is faced with religious passion that you do not understand or believe in. Be patient. *Know that whatever spiritual status a survivor is in is the only place he or she can be at this time.*

After All, It's Been Six Months, You Should Be Healed By Now

Your life can seem pretty good on most fronts except for the big gap called war. You may not feel that much different, and what I'm saying about being shattered and not knowing who you are may not seem like it applies to you. If that's the case, I want you to take some time alone to really ask yourself if you are letting yourself feel the impact. Who have you lost? What scared you the most? What has been hardest for you back home? Denial is a powerful protector, a tool for survival. It may take years before your mind lets you unwrap war's effects.

In our culture, we have little patience for wounds we cannot see, and far too little acceptance for the wounds we do see. Because of the lingering taboo over being wounded, survivors often try to hide, ignore, or deny that their wounds exist.

Yet *every* war survivor comes back with mental, emotional, spiritual and, many times, physical wounds. As I write this, more than 30,000 men and women have been sent home from Iraq and Afghanistan physically wounded. Like in most wars everywhere, they seem to exist as shadows; silent sufferers left to endure months and years of healing and adaptation to bodies they don't recognize. Quite frankly, the public doesn't want to see them. We don't want to be reminded of their sacrifices; we wouldn't know what to say.

So, we leave them to fend for themselves. That's the reality. There is very little true support for veterans—with a historically broken VA system crippled by Congress which fails to allocate the funds our troops and healing practitioners need, and a public who cringes at the thought of having to be reminded of what war does—veterans and their families are left having to fight battle after battle to get the care and acceptance that they need and deserve. Unfortunately, this probably isn't going to change anytime soon. As a survivor, you'll soon realize that this is just the way things are right now. Your healing journey is a warrior's journey; and it's going to take every ounce of strength and the support of your fellow comrades to stay on it.

Many veterans wonder if healing is actually possible. If you define healing as a return to who you were before—as if the war never happened—then, no, you can never fully heal. You cannot erase war. Healing—in the sense of creating a new sense of wholeness—*is possible*, though, if you find a way to accept your wounds and give them a place in your life.

We live in the era of the instantaneous. We want instant cures, instant fixes, instant healing. Healing rarely happens instantly. It normally takes time. It is a process. It is, in itself, a state of being. It can't be forced or rushed—not a comfort when you are hurting and desperate to find relief. Because our culture does not actively reach out and support a survivor's healing, survivors often end up reaching for the only 'relief' available: alcohol, drugs, and other addictive behaviors that temporarily numb the pain. Anyone in pain seeks relief. Families sometimes see a survivor's drinking or drug use as a moral issue, when the reality may be that survivors are trying to find some way to ease the pain and cope. If you are a survivor drinking or using, you are not alone—but without addressing your pain in ways that actually treat the wounds and not just the symptoms, your healing will be delayed and the pain will come back stronger each time you've temporarily numbed it. You have to go to the source. And you have to accept the fact that it's okay to live in a state of woundedness while allowing healing to begin.

Sadly, the spiritual and emotional wounds that survivors carry are for the most part never seen or acknowledged. War inflicts images, scents, sounds, and feelings that sear themselves into memory. These are the remnants that contort into nightmares. These are the flashes that appear at random. These are the things that haunt you. Survivors often expect to carry these wounds inside for the rest of their lives. Our belief that it's a sign of weakness to show our wounds is a tragic one. *There is no shame in being wounded. You cannot survive war without it.*

No One Knows What You Did Over There

One of the most frustrating things survivors face when they come home is the fact that no one seems to know or understand what they did "over there." The public has formed their opinion about the war and they have misperceptions and stereotypes about the roles our troops play in war. It's hard to come home and realize that no one understands and, what's more disturbing, that very, very few actually care.

Most likely, you have some very strong feelings about what really happened on the ground. You may have played a very positive role, making a true difference in the lives of civilians and your military unit. You know the combat zone quite intimately, the suffering and needs of the civilians, and you know the true value of your presence there.

As a soldier fighting in a foreign country, you became a part of that country, its memory, and legacy. Whether as invaders or freedom fighters, when soldiers enter a culture they live there. They get to know the way the sun rises on the landscape and how the weather patterns develop. They pick up some of the local language and begin to understand some of the customs, habits, and mannerisms of the culture. You may have even fallen in love or become intimate with a local who was, and may still be, surviving the war. Troops begin to identify with the people who live in their area and develop feelings for what the local civilian population is suffering.

Sadly, most Americans view the war from a distance—and few will understand how deeply you care about what happens in the country where you served. They won't "get" your attachment to the society there, your deep compassion and concern for what happens next there, or how important it is to you personally that the future in each war zone become one of peace and prosperity. The war, in that sense, will always be yours alone. You may carry a very special place in your being for the country and people you left behind—and being misunderstood or simply, not understood at all—may become a way of life for you.

I've never been able to explain my attachment to the country of Bosnia or my deep feelings for the people there—I've learned to simply not let what others think about it matter to me. It doesn't matter. I know what I know, and I feel what I feel, and it is my place in life to carry the knowledge and attachment I have for that corner of the world.

You may be tempted to try to explain to people—to convince them to care as much as you do—but I believe that while you can share what you know, you will most likely have to accept that not being understood is going to become normal. That said, don't discount what you know and the power you may have in continuing to make a difference in the land and society that you have fought for.

Why War Buddies Matter So Much

In war zones, everyone left alive is a survivor. Everyone has nightmares; everyone knows the scent of blood rising from the ground, the sounds of mortars, the echo of gunfire. In America, survivors come home to communities that do not know what they have been through. You are isolated, trapped between trying to "get over it," wanting to reconnect to loved ones, and yet probably feeling a much stronger bond with the buddies and people you left behind. The fact is that no one knows what you have been through unless they have experienced it.

That's why your combat buddies may now know you more intimately than anyone else in your life. The fact that you feel connected to men and women who had your back and fought beside you and lost the same friends you lost, is good. Shared danger bonds people more intimately than love. For months—often years—the troops in your unit have been your family. It's okay to feel close to them and it's okay to miss them. They are a vital part of who you are, and your connection with them will most likely last a lifetime. That connection—staying in touch, having reunions, emailing each other—can be a vital part of your healing journey. These people matter.

Ironically, this is something that many spouses of veterans simply do not get. Why and how could a bunch of strangers thrown together in combat mean more to your spouse than the ten years of your marriage? How is it possible that he can be so rude and heartless to you now then get all teary when he talks about his buddies? It doesn't make sense. And yet, it does. If you stop to realize that it's not the individuals themselves that he's so sensitive about (though he truly does love them); it's *why* he loves them that matters. These people know what he's been through. It's that plain and simple. They were there. You were not.

I learned to accept this early on in my marriage. I was the outsider, coming into my husband's life, and the lives of our colleagues and friends as someone untouched by war. They had a bond, one that I could not fully embrace, and one that I would never truly be a part of. They had inside jokes, memories they shared of survival; I could only listen and imagine. My husband loves me completely, but there are people in his life who have a place in him that I do not own, and that's okay. There is space in his heart for me, for the war, and for his close friends. Who says we have to own all of someone's heart to be fully theirs?

Don't be jealous of your survivor's relationship with the *men and women who helped keep him alive.* Give thanks for these people. They carried your spouse and are a part of him now. Don't compare your relationship to your survivor with his relationship to his buddies. He doesn't love these people more than he loves you or your family, but he does love them. It's just a different kind of love and different type of relationship. And yes, it is emotionally intimate. War does that. He's going to think about them; he's going to worry about them; he's going to feel at times much closer to them than he does to you.

Make room in your heart for these people—the war buddies. Allow them in. They can help you know how to relate to your survivor. They can fill in gaps. They can help you understand just how resilient and human your loved one is.

Of course, it's understandable that as a spouse you want to be everything your survivor needs. You want to draw closer, to become a part of that world, to have your love be enough. And that's an expectation spouses often have— that their love is, or should be, enough to heal. No doubt, your love is a vital, vital part; but it is not enough.

As a loving partner, one of the most important gifts you need to give to yourself right now is to let go of the weight you carry for your survivor's recovery. *You cannot heal your war survivor.* He or she has the resiliency, the inner strength that has the potential to eventually knit scar tissue over the wounds and lessen the pain. Your gift is acceptance. Acceptance is one of the most crucial healing factors a war survivor needs. By accepting the fact that you are not responsible for healing war wounds and that you are not *able* to heal war wounds, you will open up loving space that will encompass your survivor, help him or her to feel safe to be who they are, and face an uncertain future.

Expectations abound about life after war. People assume how things will be, and while they mean well, much of their assumptions are based on their own fear of facing change. People want war survivors and their families to be the same as they were. We don't want to face the reality that people we send to war come back different, and that those who are left behind change. We don't want to deal with the uncertainty and the insecurity that comes from the unknown. We're scared of losing what is familiar; and losing the familiar in a loved one is one of the scariest things to face.

Nevertheless, we have to let go of the expectation that those impacted by war will someday be the same as they were before war. This is part of what families and societies lose in war, and it's a deep loss. War takes parts of our loved ones away from us. It takes time from our lives, robs children of their parents, robs parents of their children, and leaves families to survive through incredible fear and suspense.

War is not an event that can be experienced and forgotten. It changes who people are, and it becomes a part of you. War will be a part of your lives for the rest of your life.

Voices

Home: Day One

I started down from the steps of the plane, looking around to try to spot her. Not hard at all: around five-feet, nine-inches, very voluptuous, but at eighteen, just out of high school, and almost through Cosmetology College.

She was screaming "Tom, Tom, over here, Darling!" and running towards me. God, she was, and probably still is, beautiful. (Side note: I *still* love her.)

She jumped into my arms, and we went home to start a "normal" life. But in my case, how do you do that—as I had re-enlisted in the Army to get the money to marry her. We had a connection on a couple of dates before I left for Vietnam, and during correspondence (assuming we were both telling the truth) we had fallen in love, and become engaged.

So, things rolled along, and we got married, and went and used my "blood money"—as I thought of it—as a down payment on a two-bed trailer home. Many soldiers and their wives were what some called "Trailer Trash" but it *was* a start. Due to the permissive society we lived in, we had gone on a drive one time to Pagago Park, it was almost sunset, we had been talking, and all of a sudden, she said:

"Love me, Tom," and, well, what could I say or do, but what I felt?

The day they delivered our trailer—a beautiful twelve-by-sixty foot, two bedroom, freshly bought with a VA loan—we showed up to move in on the last week or so of my post-Vietnam leave. We had *not* been sleeping together. Her father, a 1st Cavalry Division veteran of the Pacific war in WWII would not hear of it, and I *respected that*. We basically had that one slip in Papago Park; but, in all honesty, we had some "plans" after that, though we were staying in the same house, in separate bedrooms.

Yeah, I know the setup to this story is a little long, but it relates to understanding the rest of it. A hot and horny young warrior back from the war, and a hot and horny babe anxious to be married and start what was supposed to be the "perfect life."

On night one, I felt I owed it to her to explain to her a crucial point based on the story of the tunnels of Cu-Chi. We did not know it at the time, but I still needed to relate to her the story of how the people who oriented us as we came into Vietnam had mentioned that there had been soldiers found with their throats cut. They told us we needed a "password" to get back into the "Hootches" we lived in after dark, or we could end up dead. Then, after I moved up to Dau-Tieng, and began going out on combat operations with a direct support artillery outfit, it became real one night, as I was on perimeter guard, and we were hearing reports about possible enemy infiltration through the perimeter from our "listening post" outposts.

Bottom line: I had to try to explain to her that I slept in hyper-paranoid mode, and *under no circumstances* was she to touch me anywhere, except in drill instructor mode: tap the bottom of my foot, or whack it. She could not get it. She did not *want* to get it. It was just too horrible for her to contemplate, and eventually, it ended in our divorce. I cannot count how many hundreds of times she forgot what I reminded her of every single day: while I am asleep do *not* touch me anywhere, but on the bottom of my foot, drill-instructor-style.

And the poor beautiful baby only wanted to wake me up passionately and lovingly to a brand new, shiny day, with some love, and maybe even some sex, and instead I had the guilt of waking up with her throat in my hands, and her eyes bulging in horror, because in my unconscious mind, I was fighting for my life against a Sapper. Her mother and father thought I abused her, because, and like the beautiful loving person she was, she insisted on trying to throw her arms around me, saying "Welcome me to another morning of love between us."

I tried and tried, but she just could not get it. She did not want to contemplate or understand such horrible things. To *get* it. Double emphasis, I know, but important enough to be double. And the worst part was—she tried to tell them there was no abuse, but "Daddy's Little Girl" could not possibly be to blame for that. And of course, that is partly true, though, it was not really her, but the mindset of Middle American womanhood.

The guilt—the good part is that eventually, my guilt forced behavior changes and it ended, but the damage had been done.

After years of bitterness about why "they" did not understand, I finally realized that there was no possible way we could possibly expect them to.

Not only were they unable to—they did not want to.

But then, the next revelation was: hell, they are just like me! I do not want to understand it, or know it, either! My kingdom for a memory eraser! What kingdom? Okay, my ratty little trailer, and my lousy seven-dollars-per-hour job. Anything! Only take the weight off! *Let me live again!*

—a Vietnam veteran and PTSD survivor (name withheld for privacy)

What's Running Through My Mind Now...

2

Talking About War

✦

How do you talk about war?

For war survivors and loving families, knowing what to say or how to say it can be overwhelming. Do you talk about the war? Do you ask him what it was like? Isn't it best if he shares all that stuff with you? Or should you just leave him alone?

Survivors wonder, too. They balk at the idea of talking about gruesome experiences. They live with the images in their mind and dreams; putting it into words just relives it. And then there is the fear of breaking the precious innocence that loved ones have intact. Survivors wonder: Will people still love me if they know what I know? Will they still love me if they knew what I had to do to survive? Would they still love me if they saw the dark side of me that I saw? Would they want me sitting at the dinner table if they knew the stuff crawling through my mind?

Much of war gets trampled underneath when a soldier comes home. The initial homecoming period wears off, spouses become casual again, the energy of the home moves back to daily routines, paying bills, and social demands. Survivors who may feel like talking often remain silent, not wanting to disrupt things, and afraid of how loved ones will respond. They may just want to put things behind them. Spouses feel uncertain of what to say, how much to say, or even if they really want to know. Survivors soon get trapped in a cocoon of isolation that is both comforting and extremely lonely.

Should you talk about the war?

Yes.

Why? Because sharing pain, guilt, loss, fear, uncertainty, and what it was like breaks the isolation survivors live in, and lets others in to support healing. War isn't meant to be carried alone.

How do you talk about war?

There is no easy way. And there are no rules. What I have found is that war is so big and so deep and so intimately experienced that only when we have a profound *respect* for a survivor's pain, can we give them the kind of open acceptance that fosters sharing.

That means the pain has to be sacred ground. Not a space to be trampled on, dragged out, or examined under a microscope. Not a place for merely the curious. A survivor's war is sacred ground. The naked ground where life and death have been faced, met, and known. The survivor is the only one who has the right to touch that ground.

Survivors need to believe they are safe and accepted to invite you into their war-ground. And you need a reason to be there. If genuine compassion and support aren't your motivating factors, then you have no reason to ask and no right to listen. Imagine, for a moment, the most embarrassing, painful, or humiliating experience you've ever had. Something you wouldn't want anyone you love to know. Now imagine sharing it with your spouse who was not there, didn't know you then, and has no way of knowing all the little details that surrounded the experience to make it more understandable. Imagine talking about this openly. Who would you trust? The people closest to us are the ones we are most afraid to share our secrets with. Why? Because it involves the most risk. Can you see then why a spouse may be the hardest person for a survivor to share an experience with? What loved ones think matters most. Your opinion outweighs everything else. You have the ability to reject him or her and risking that rejection may not be worth it. They'd rather suffer in silence. (Another reason survivors turn to war buddies. There's no fear of rejection.)

Survivors wonder who to trust. How do you know who really is supportive of you, who can handle it? How do you know if they will still accept you once they know how things really were?

Look for someone who has some familiarity with war, death, and suffering. Someone who knows how to listen. Consider the person's motivation. Why do they want to listen to you? Have they offered? What would they be able to do with the information? How would knowing about your pain change your relationship with them? Have they been supportive of you in the past? Do they have some background that gives them insight into what you might be going through?

It may not be anyone in your family. It may be a friend. You may want to start with a trauma therapist. Contact a hospital and ask to speak with a grief counselor. They may be able to connect you with people who are genuinely caring and receptive. Or, perhaps you may feel safest by just starting to Blog or journal your experiences in private. Visit http://www.lifeafterwar.org for more information on writing your experiences.

Bottom line: the people a survivor trusts with war experiences need to show a history of being extremely patient, openly caring, non-judgmental, and willing to face the dark. There is no other way to put hell into words.

Survivors, and those who care, need the *courage and support to talk about war and face its reality.* Our society is terrified of death and generally inept at dealing with true emotional pain. How ironic that we are addicted to the television crime show, *CSI*, but, god forbid, we sit down with a soldier and openly discuss what seeing real dead bodies and mutilation does to the soul. We need to be shouldering the emotional and spiritual pain of war with our troops. We expect our soldiers to kill people for us, then come home and carry that weight on their conscience alone. Why?

Soldiers are not individuals who have acted according to their own personal goals. They belong to each of us as citizens of this country. We've lost this sense because our military is an all-volunteer force. Instead of seeing our troops as people who belong to us, *people we are responsible for,* we tend to see them as a private force, almost as an independent profession—like investigators or journalists—people who have chosen a job that puts them in danger. It's true that today's soldier has his or her own personal reasons for enlisting, but the profession itself exists for the sake of every other American who never does. We cannot separate soldiers from ourselves and expect them to be there when we need them.

Sensing that troops are ours, collectively, gets even more complicated when the wars we fight do not touch the homeland and the intent behind them is questioned. The missions we've sent our National Guard troops on in recent years, for instance, have turned America's concept of military service into a half-humanitarian, half-defender role. Without the sense that troops are putting themselves in direct danger *so that we don't have to be,* we start to see them, again, as a separate force that goes off on isolated missions to far away places around the world. We do not feel the national unification that past wars have created when our national security was clearly at stake. It's too easy to see Iraq as "Bush's war" rather than "our war," or to see Afghanistan as some extended operation in an obscure locale where troops encounter men in turbans and chase terrorists through caves. We do not sense that these missions impact our everyday lives. And for many Americans, the first time the war becomes real to them is when a veteran in their community comes home.

It's hard to accept, but many people simply don't want to know. And as a survivor, you're going to run into this. People don't want to hear about war, to see its reality, or deal with the trauma. They're goodhearted people, but they don't know how to deal with it—and so, they don't.

As one veteran told me, "I had people and relatives I didn't even know sending me letters while I was in Iraq. But when I got home, everyone disappeared."

The war doesn't end when troops come home. It's *after* war when troops need the most support.

Unfortunately, how well returning troops are received when they come home also depends on how the nation generally feels about the war. Unpopular wars have turned our troops into outcasts to be shunned, humiliated, and ridiculed. Ignored wars turn our troops into shadows that suffer in silence.

Unless we change our attitude as a society and separate our sentiment about the politics of war from our respect for soldiers themselves, our troops will never feel the support they need to recover from war. It starts with individuals. With loving families and caring friends who find the courage to overcome the fear and awkwardness of talking about war and really take on the burden of sharing its horror. We owe this to our troops. It's the only way survivors will find the support and psychic relief to begin the healing process.

So how do you, actually, talk about war?

For loving families and friends, it starts with an understanding that you're going to have to get your hands dirty, or in this case, your soul. In order for a survivor to share what they've been through they have to believe that you are strong enough to carry it. Survivors do not want to expose people to the horrors of war. They are generally very sensitive to what you will think of them if you know the truth. By letting them know of your genuine support and willingness to talk about severed heads and what it feels like to have someone's brains on your skin—you give them a safe place to unload some of the trauma they're trying to carry alone. And they need to know that war is not something they have to carry alone. We need to carry it with them.

It takes courage to open yourself to this kind of exposure and this knowledge. You need to ask yourself if it's something you can really handle knowing. Can you even say the words— "severed head"—out loud? Can you watch a graphic war movie? Graphic images, accounts of death, killing and the little details speak volumes to what a survivor has been through. Even just talking about war in general, the missions troops were on, their daily routine can help a soldier feel a bit more understood.

One caution: learning about war will create uncomfortable emotions and, in effect, raise some of the same issues in you that your survivor is dealing with. Some people fear (and survivors have this particular concern) that if stories of war are openly revealed, the hearer will also become traumatized. There is some truth to that, because any exposure to war will change you. Are we taking a risk to our own well-being by hearing what our survivors have endured? Perhaps. But it is our duty to share this with them. Every war we fight is *our war*—not just theirs. Why shouldn't we also be affected by its horror? Only when we share the emotional and spiritual trauma of war do we, as a country, begin to understand what war is, and whether or not we delve into it again the same way in the future. We begin to get a grasp on what it does, what it means, and gain insight into the deeper questions in life that war so acutely raises. And we begin to share the burden of taking life.

Getting Graphic

Do we really need to know and discuss the graphic details? Yes. But this isn't about being exposed to guts and blood and death for its own sake. Survivors are worried you'll judge them and they're judging themselves a million times harder than you ever will. This isn't about graphic stories that make you want to vomit. This is about *validating* a survivor's experience so that he or she can be more fully known and understood.

Survivors deserve to be known—not just as 'Joe who came back from the war and just isn't the same'—but as 'Joe who saw his best friend's legs blown off, had to watch him bleed to death, and that's why he isn't the same.' Survivors need acceptance; plain and simple. I can't say it enough. It is the most important gift you can give. They need to know even in their pain, their nightmares, their PTSD reactions, their seeming insanity at times—that they are fundamentally okay. Accepted. Wanted. Believed. They deserve long-term patience and assurances of support.

If you don't think you can hear what your survivor has to say without judging him or her for it, or without denying the true pain of it, then you are not yet ready to hear what a survivor has to share. Trust is a huge issue. Relationships are complicated. Survivors need to discern who is safe and who is merely curious, but unable to handle the truth.

If you are ready, tell your survivor you are here for them if he or she wants to talk about what they saw and felt and went through. From the beginning of our relationship, I've continually offered to be there for my husband if and when he feels like sharing his war. Like many survivors, and men in particular, he doesn't talk a lot about his feelings. But, over time, bits and pieces have emerged. We cry together when a memory, song, or a news-replay brings back a flood of unexpected emotion. Sometimes I just hold him and listen to everything that's not being said in our understanding that war is simply a part of our lives.

I've learned to be open and pay attention to those times when a comment or insight into a survivor's world is shared. Listen hard and show affection. Cry, if that's what it does to you. Seeing you appropriately react emotionally to trauma can help a survivor reconnect inside with his or her own reaction or lack of one. Let your survivor know that you aren't afraid to talk about the ugly stuff. Bring up graphic terms first, talk about it matter-of-factly, ask tough questions. Let him or her know that you can handle it. Don't make it a big deal. Talk about it as if it were just everyday life. Be frank. Be bold. Be curious. Be courageous. And let yourself feel the reaction it evokes in you—you'll get a microscopic glimpse into what your survivor lives with every day and every night.

Talking about war is not easy. It hurts to hear it, and it hurts to feel it. Realistically, we should all be hurt by the wars our soldiers fight. We should all have to live with some of the pain that we expect them to shoulder. And we should be the first in line to take them aside and let them know that they are not alone, that we are going to walk with them through this for the rest of their lives. That we understand that killing another human being on our behalf is a spiritual burden we must also bear.

Being willing to listen and openly ask questions does not mean that you should pressure a survivor to talk. Remember, this is sacred ground. As a loving family or friend, you must remember that *talking about war does not erase war*. It does not necessarily heal wounds or make anything better. Don't fall prey to the hope that talking is an instant cure, and that once it's done and over with, everything will return to normal. War is part of who a survivor is—as much a part of him as his childhood. It can be distanced, processed, understood, examined, accepted, but it will never be gone.

Even though war should be society's shared wound, it's important to realize, too, that war is intimately personal. How a survivor feels about his role and what he has experienced needs to be treated with reverence. Respecting traumatic pain as a part of him that simply is—not pitied, not played down, not ignored—will help a survivor validate his own experience. Soldiers are tough and they live in a military culture that demands they be tough and not show any signs of weakness. It can be a bitter internal battle for soldiers to try to figure out how to reconcile what they feel inside with how they are supposed to behave on the outside. Sometimes the hardest part is convincing themselves that it's okay to feel hurt, to feel sad, to not feel okay with what they have experienced. When loving friends and family behave as if feeling hurt and confused is *normal and to be expected*, then soldiers can begin to relax a bit and start to accept their woundedness.

As a family or friend, you may find yourself overwhelmed by the stories you hear, or by imagining what it must have been like. Be overwhelmed. Respond emotionally. This is your pain now, too. Some of what a survivor may talk about may not make sense to you. They cannot fully share what things were really like. It's not possible. There literally are no words for some things. Keep in mind, too, that survivors live with a different concept of reality than you do. Americans are generally very either/or people. Things are black and white. Good or bad. True or false. Good guys versus bad guys. In the chaos of war and the spiritual crisis it creates, these clear lines blur fast. Remember, as you relate to a survivor, that there is no one truth. Truth is a perception based on personal experience and interpretation. Everybody has their own version—or multiple versions of truth. There is a place for duality of thoughts and beliefs. Be open to stretching your own beliefs as you learn more about the experiences your survivor has had.

The Survivor's Side

As a survivor, the idea of talking about your experience may be appalling, to say the least. Many survivors do not want to and will not talk about it. Thrown into isolation at home, and with little access to your combat buddies, toughening up and shutting up are normal responses. If you're a man, you may not see any reason at all to talk about what you feel—and that's okay, men generally don't think in terms of feelings. But you do think in terms of experiences and what things were like and you experience emotions in many ways. Loss, fear, grief, disbelief, disappointment, shame, humiliation, anger, joy, elation—you may not have ready words for what you feel, and what you feel may come across in how much energy you have, your temperament, and your reactions to others. Don't be convinced by society that you shouldn't talk about what war felt like, and still feels like to you. War is emotional. Perhaps what is most important for you, as a man, is that you find some way to express what's going on inside of you in a way that isn't destructive to you or anyone else. If you're lucky enough to have a partner or best friend who is a woman, she has incredible natural abilities to help you figure out what you're feeling and lead you to understand how your emotions impact your life.

If you are a female survivor, you're probably more inclined to talk about how you feel. I know, from my experience, getting overwhelmed by more emotions than I knew how to handle made my journey that much more difficult. I felt layered emotions—dark, ugly, menacing ones that I didn't know how to deal with. I'm quite reserved and generally don't talk about what I'm feeling. Instead, I write, and it's an effective way for me as it serves my life and others. However, not talking about what I went through in Bosnia kept me isolated inside. No one knew my inner conflict, you wouldn't have been able to tell how shattered I felt—except for the fact that privately I cried easily and often. Women usually have a need to express our feelings, if for no other reason than to clarify them to ourselves—but trauma can be incredibly silencing. And suddenly not having words can make you feel stuck inside yourself.

For both men and women, it may seem that there simply are no words for what you've seen, heard, felt, done, and lived with. Some things are just too gruesome for our minds to formulate into words and express. *That's okay.* What you need to understand is that what is in you is looking for release, looking for a way out of you, looking for another person of energy who can carry its weight and impact with you. When it is locked inside it grows in power. It becomes larger and stronger and wilder. Releasing it in some form of expression diminishes its power, and cuts it back down to size.

You don't have to use words to talk about the war. Paint. Draw. Take photos. From art therapy, music, to simply taking up an old (or new) creative hobby, anything that reconnects you with creative activity may help you express your war and see it in a new way.

Be aware of the tendency to fall back on the thought that you are tough (which you are), and that carrying war around in you is just part of being a soldier. *You need to realize that you have the right to share this with someone you trust.* No matter how dark or sick or repulsive the thoughts and images pulsing through you are, they are normal for someone who has been through what you have. You are not the only one experiencing this. And no, you are not insane. What you have to say may be horrifying, but it is not something that no one has heard before. It's okay to talk about it. There is a web of compassion around you—you may have to look outside your normal circle to find it, but there are compassionate people out there who are willing and able to listen to you. As hard as it may be, you owe it to yourself to put as much effort into fighting to heal as you did in fighting to stay alive.

You may never feel ready to talk about the war. You may never feel comfortable with the idea of sharing the horror. But, if you can, don't be afraid to tell it like it is and like it was. It may seem that talking about your war experiences victimizes those who listen. Or that you will be re-traumatized. Remember, there is a big difference between experiencing what you have (which is how you experience your story—in vivid, sensual memories) and listening to it as a story. The details and events may be shocking to your listener, but they will not feel the fear, the physical sensations, the actual circumstances that all played in to how you experienced it.

When you are ready to share, trust yourself. Your spirit knows what you need to heal. When you are ready to learn from hearing yourself tell your own story, you will do so. You may be ready days after you get home, or it may take you years to come to that place, and either way, it's all right.

Sasha and I have had the advantage of having written about war for years; and, in essence have had many of our own feelings about it expressed by giving others a voice. But there is always something ready to bring it to the surface again. I made up my mind when I married him that I was not going to try to change him. War is sacred, and I know that it is possible to arrive at a place where you can both dwell with the memories and experience happiness and fulfillment at the same time.

Just remember that there is intense power in storytelling. Whether it's told to another person or written down in words, storytelling unleashes the power to give meaning to life, and helps you create a new perspective. What is locked inside of you is, in its essence, more image than story. Images, scents, sights, sounds, tastes, thrills, lows, sensations that were captured in your adrenaline-spiked photographic memory. Taking those images and putting words to them can empower you.

What is trapped in your spirit will not take its place in history until it's released. Expressing your stories gives you back some measure of control. Releasing those experiences and energies back into the vastness of the Universe will allow the Universe to swallow them up and breathe the softness of life back into you. One breath at a time. It will also allow you to see your experiences *as a story*—and, with insight, allow you to choose to see your story from a new perspective. Our experiences are stories—stories that our minds create based on our past experiences, our beliefs, and what we expect life to be like. Our stories incorporate facts, but they are still stories. That's why two people can witness the same event and give very different accounts of what happened. It's because our minds create or assign meaning to experiences based on who we are at that point in our lives. When you tell your war stories, and especially when you gather with others who shared your experiences, you will often find that other people's stories shine light on your own. They help you to see differently. They expand the sense of meaning that you've created. And they allow you to look at what happened from a new vantage point—from who you are today. Facts cannot be changed, but how we feel about those facts can. What we believe leads to our thoughts, and our thoughts lead to our feelings. Our feelings are how we experience our world. When you change what you believe, your thoughts change, and so do your feelings. You create a new experience of reality.

Telling your story is not easy; and it's not something you may feel like doing. But it is a powerful step toward healing. It brings you back from a sense of isolation and reconnects you with the rest of humanity. It reminds you that you are part of a whole, interconnected with all humans, including those you have killed, those you have lost, those you wish you could get back, and those you wish you could still kill. It also allows those who love you to support your healing, and it lets us carry the burden of war together.

Voices

Clean Up on Aisle 6

Cheerios could be so cruel. The yellow cardboard containers of boyhood grinned at her from the shelves.

She had just tossed the unopened box that had sat all these months on the kitchen counter, to be seen and to be there, when he walked through the door. A bright, cheery, yellow box for him to know he was home again.

It was a talisman for them both. As long as the Cheerios box was on the counter, it meant he would come home, safe and sound. The yellow cardboard would protect him.

She held the box, cradled it like a newborn, hugging the happy oats as she checked her list and headed for the frozen food aisle.

Staring at the frozen corn and Chicken Pot Pies in the frosty bin, she heard that sound again. Still as a gravestone, she waited—a hollow plopping sound jerked her eyes to the right. Nothing. Another hollow plop-plop echo. She looked left. Nothing.

Chicken Pot Pie, his favorite fast food. Pop it in the microwave, nuke it for five minutes, and scarf it down on his way to the second of his two-a-day football practice sessions. He was always on his way somewhere, or the universal 'nowhere' destination of school boys. She grabbed several boxes and dropped them in her cart, a growing pile of resurrection food.

She heard it again. Plop-plop.

This time she caught it, right in front of her face. She looked down. The front side of the yellow Cheerios box, face up in her arms, with that happy oat smile of goodness, was speckled with teardrops.

She pinched her eyes to stop the tears and scurried out of the store.

The manager scowled as he rounded the corner and spotted the abandoned wire cart in the middle of Aisle 6. He scanned the area for the owner, but found no one. He sighed as he grabbed the cart, "Inconsiderate and just plain rude," he told himself. "A half-filled cart, with a pile of nearly thawed Chicken Pot Pies, all left for someone else to clean up. What's wrong with people?"

He stooped to pick up a tear-stained grocery list stuck to a photo, on the floor. A picture of a mother and her soldier-son: mom clutching his arm with a frozen smile as the boy tried to look grown-up in a fresh green uniform.

His eyes fixed on the yellow Cheerios box, warped and crushed and dented, as though someone had squeezed the life out of it. He brushed the water spots with his palm.

He knew he'd have to stick the Cheerios and everything else in the storeroom, on the spoilage rack. A waste. "Didn't folks understand? It was just cardboard. Cardboard was flimsy. Cardboard didn't protect anything."

—John Cory

What's Running Through My Mind Now...

3

Where the Soul Goes

✦

"I feel as if my soul has been sliced open. Every ounce of good, of faith, of life, of hope is gushing out and *nothing is stopping it*. I want to be whole, to heal, to find meaning, but there is—*nothing*."

I wrote that in my diary in Sarajevo in 2002, two years after I had moved there. The war had been over since 1995, but it might as well have ended the day before my plane landed. The peace agreement that had ended the war seemed to have also frozen time. The fighting had stopped, but in many ways the war hadn't. The city was quiet, dazed, buildings splattered with thousands of bullet pock marks; you could see through what once had been office buildings by way of the huge, gaping holes in their sides. Still active land mines remained throughout former frontlines within the city. NATO-led peacekeepers patrolled regularly. People were still holding their breath, waiting to see if the war would start up again.

Intuition had told me, when I first arrived, that the "radiation" of war would kill me, slowly, one devastating story at a time. But it didn't stop me. I stayed. From the time I was seventeen, I had sensed, by some uncanny intuition, that I was meant to live in Bosnia. And I was right. I knew before I ever got there that Sarajevo would feel like home. It did, and it still does. It's where my soul has its deepest connection, unearthed and lived with the deepest questions, has been loved the most, and where in a journey that wouldn't let me go I nearly became lost forever.

People who haven't been to a post-war city often have the impression that it's very exotic. They don't realize that when you are living there—life isn't that much different than anywhere else. You eat, you sleep, you make love, you laugh, you work, you find friends, you get sick, you go shopping; you think that because the conflict is "over" that you are insulated from war. What you don't realize in the midst of all that, though, is that unlike places where the spirit and energy of war has not touched every single thing in the environment, war seeps in and takes over your soul. You're not immune and there is no protection. When you live in a place that holds the energy of war, that energy affects you.

When you come home from war, you carry that energy of war in you, and it starts to impact those around you and your environment. I believe that many times family and loved ones tend to blame the survivor for negative effects after war, when in reality, they should be blaming the energy of war. This energy will remain in your soul until it is recognized for what it is, and released.

The energy of war shakes the very essence of our being down to our innermost core, and that core is our soul. It's the spirit part of us that knows we have existed on some spiritual level long before we entered the world; and knows, too, that when our body dies, we still exist. Nearly every religion holds the concept of the soul as a separate entity from the physical body. Most people, at some point, instinctively feel this. Our soul is who we relate to when we are in ourselves. It is the part of us that holds the emotions created by the chemicals in our brains, and the underlying essence behind our thoughts and motivations. It is the mystical, magical, mysterious part of us that life on earth never explains.

It is our most fundamental essence and where the energy of life resides.

Your soul cannot be killed. It cannot die, but it can leave the body. When the energy of war (death) enters your soul, it creates a deep sense of dis-ease. The life energy in your soul knows that the death energy of war is not meant to be part of the soul. It doesn't belong there. This is where the internal conflict begins to take place. This is why people exposed to war naturally talk about war in terms of what it has done to their soul.

War goes straight for the soul. The energy of war invades and overtakes. It consumes. It splits the soul into fragments. The soul becomes uncertain of its presence here on earth, and in the repeated, prolonged exposure to impending death that combat survivors endure, the soul remains on the constant verge of leaving. Some combat survivors actually experience their soul leaving their body, despite not being physically killed. They can pinpoint the time and location when it happened.

Few ever talk about this, but it does happen. For war survivors, admitting that you feel you no longer have a soul can be terrifying. You wonder if what you feel is real, and if others will think you're insane. You're not. If this is your experience, please know that what you are feeling is real and valid and there is hope for getting your soul back. You are not dead despite your gut feeling that you are.

Dr. Edward Tick, a compassionate therapist who has helped veterans find wholeness and healing for over twenty years, has written about war's effect on the soul in his book, *War and the Soul*. His website, http://www.soldiersheart.net can help connect you to people who can assist you in the process of inviting your soul back into your body. Do not give up hope, no matter how long you have felt that your soul has been gone.

Losing Your Soul

Having your soul leave is the ultimate price to pay as a survivor. More commonly, survivors have a sense of 'losing their soul.' What we actually mean is that we are losing our *identity or parts of us that we never wanted to lose.*

When war destroys everything human beings consider 'normal' it cracks the foundation of our identity. Every war survivor—and even people like me who have only lived intimately with the aftermath of war—goes through a deep identity transformation. You are essentially stripped down to your most basic being and left to slowly sift and sort and try to find pieces that will fit the "after war" person you are becoming. What you once believed is no longer solid. Questions about who you are, the meaning of life, spirituality, good and evil, safety, security, the future, goals, and priorities—all of these get shaken.

With the intense survival mode of the battlefield gone, and the sudden absence of impending death, you are left with wounds and questions percolating inside you. You come back to a world that has not changed in the way you have. A world that still hangs on to its religion, order, routines, priorities, and concept of what it means to be alive. This is not the world that you know now—even if you desperately want it to be. Your world—your concept of daily life, has been radically altered.

Feeling like you are losing, or have lost, your soul is normal. It can feel like you are hollow inside, disconnected, uncertain, or confused. Seeing everyone else around you living "normal American lives" and walking around worried about stupid, petty problems—the kind of problems they should get down on their knees and thank God for—only leads to a further sense of isolation. Is there anyone who understands you now? Many war survivors will try to suppress what's going on inside of them in order to try to 'fit' back into the world of home.

It doesn't work.

War levels us to the ground and in the process, brings us back to a very simple basis of life. It's gift—if we may frame it that way—is that in the end it gives us the chance to dig deeper and redefine life in a way that may be more humane, compassionate, and accepting toward all humanity. It re-invites us to connect with our essence as human beings. In our concept of 'losing our souls' we may, actually, find them.

It's much easier to write or read about this than to live through it. The questions are dark and the void may seem bottomless. Without the comfort of formerly held beliefs, we feel stranded in mid-air with no ground underneath. Whatever concept of security we took for granted seems destroyed.

There is no longer any protection. In its purest form, this creates a drive to cherish life, to live in the moment, to never take anything for granted. In its darkest form, this creates an endless pit of fear that we are constantly losing what we hold dear to us, and that fate is just waiting to strike. A certainty that nothing is ever certain.

In Bosnia, the one thing I held onto was my faith in the love I shared with Sasha, and the joy I discovered in our newborn son. That love was pure, it existed, I could believe in that. In fact, the birth of our son was what prompted me to really pay attention to what was going on in my soul. It woke me up. I had a precious, innocent child. A child untouched by war and I couldn't imagine being a mother as a cynical, disbelieving, angry woman who had no faith in good or God. Who would teach my child to love life if I didn't? Who would teach my son that there is life and healing after war? That while war was part of his history, it was not his heritage? I wanted him to find joy in life, to have faith in people, to believe that good exists. And if I couldn't give him that, then who would? My motivation to find healing became almost desperate. I *had* to find answers.

So the journey to find a new sense of wholeness began. And it continues to this day. One of the most solid pieces fell into place through writing this book: a sense of purpose for what I've been through, and a deep, abiding belief in spiritual wholeness.

My journey has not been easy, and for those who have actually been through war itself, it is a million times harder. With the intensity of war's trauma, you may be left with very little to hold onto. Without something to give context to your life, you may find yourself living in a world that has no meaning, few restraints, and even, perhaps, a blatant disregard for life.

It's hard for loving families and friends to understand this, but once the threshold of taking life is crossed there is really little else that can matter—until the soul finds itself again.

A Soldier's Conscience

How combat survivors feel about taking life is part of how war impacts the soul. Soldiers are stripped of their individuality in order to become systematic killers. They are not supposed to have a conscience, and yet, of course, they do. In today's military, where soldiers deployed are often used simultaneously to kill and heal in the same society, the lines become very gray.

Take, for instance, the soldiers who were on patrol in Baghdad on June 18, 2007, and came upon dozens of starving, abused children, tied up like dogs, baking in the 120-degree heat. These men and women are required one moment to have the absence of human empathy to gun down Iraqi insurgents and, in the next, feel deep compassion to rescue Iraqi children. These troops are caring dads and moms, brothers and sisters, sons and daughters who do their best to hang onto the softness needed to care. As one soldier said, rescuing those children made his entire tour worthwhile.[3]

My point is, the dual-purpose expectations we have of our troops create even more emotional and psychic conflict than what has traditionally been a soldier's role: to kill the enemy. Today's soldiers are meant to kill when they have to, help when they can—often the same people who may or may not be trying to kill them. To come out of this kind of situation and have a solid sense of justification for what you were required to do is very, very difficult.

We socially demand that soldiers no longer 'lose their humanity,' and without that allowance, killing becomes far more difficult to accept. This may be one reason why more soldiers are taking their own lives than being killed in battle. Soldiers are, after all, decent human beings who uphold strong benevolent morals. The current generation of soldiers has been raised to be more openly sensitive, connected to their humanity, and global-minded. (This may be a sign of progress for humanity in general, but it doesn't help at all when it comes to war.) Soldier's care, they give, and they don't like hurting people. They never have and they never will. We've asked our soldiers to be caring warriors—and that makes it hard for soldiers to create a sense of identity that morally allows for killing.

In order to live with the aftermath of war, survivors have to have a strong sense of justification for what they were asked and required to do on the battlefield. This comes down to the purpose of war. Why are we fighting? Troops may go into war with a strong sense of altruistic purpose; to free a country from an evil dictator; to spread democracy (our way of life that we believe works best in giving people human rights); or in general, freeing people from tyranny, inhumane treatment; or from war itself (peacekeeping). These purposes, while passionate, are not enough to override the human resistance to taking life. You have to perceive a direct threat to your own safety and security.

Defending our country, our national ideals, our American way of life are deeper reasons that help justify taking life in war. The more personal the threat, though—for instance, if an army was invading the United States and our individual homes and families were directly threatened—the more solid and compelling justification we would feel for killing the enemy. And the easier it would be for survivors to accept their role in war after they return home.

Psychologically, troops must feel a strong sense of mission in order to carry out their duties. The lower the personal threat, the higher the risk of losing that sense of mission. When the purpose of a war is called into question at home, troops begin to lose the defining mission that keeps them going. When a country isn't heartily behind a war, it does not value its soldiers or support and respect their willingness to kill. Instead, the controversy and lack of purpose the country feels is often taken out on returning soldiers with either anger or indifference. *Despite the fact that soldiers perform their duty as they would in any war.*

Soldiers in the field are insulated by the immediate engagement of war, but lack of support back home does trickle down. The longer a war goes on, and the longer troops are on the battlefield, the more questions and doubts begin to rise. Morale plummets as troops try to hold on to what may no longer be a clearly defined purpose. One Vietnam veteran I know told me that after awhile, the war became purely a mission to survive—that was the only thing he and his squad lived for, and that was what kept them going. There was no purpose or sense of mission for them.

Lack of support leads to deeper questions. Questions about whether or not the larger intention of the war is altruistic or merely committed for the interest of a few; questions about whether or not victory is possible, and even what the definition of success is or should be. These questions and the once-clear lines that become distorted and uncertain, can all lead a soldier to self-loathing if he is commanded to kill when he no longer is sure why the person on the other end of his weapon must die. This self-loathing can lead to a sensation that you are killing or must kill your own soul in exchange for killing others. To civilians back home, the enemy is a faceless image—a name;

to soldiers in battle, the enemy are real men, women, and often children, who not only are very real, but sometimes even quite likeable. They're human. Soldiers end up knowing that "the enemy" are real people, just like us. In wars where the enemy doesn't look any different from the civilian population, it's hard to decipher who to feel compassion for and who to harden your heart against because you might have to kill them. As survivors try to make sense of it all, their souls are deeply involved and impacted by what they have to do to survive and to accomplish the orders they're given. They are in essence trading their souls to survive.

War—killing, death and near-death—are events that affect whether or not a human soul remains present or returns to the spiritual realm. Survivors have dealt in this realm, trading life for death, making life and death decisions, and bear the heaviest weight of humanity's collective conscience. Yet, as citizens of the same country, we each need to bear this weight on our souls.

Dealing with the Souls of the Dead

Many war survivors believe that when it's your time to die, you die. That there is some Higher Power that has already determined when that time will come and that you are powerless to change it. It simply is. This is harder to hold on to when it comes to the death of children, but, for the sake of this point, let's assume that this concept is true. That a Spiritual force is determining when souls enter and leave life on earth.

If this is true, then the souls that you have killed would also fall into this concept. In other words, it was simply their 'time' to leave life on earth and reenter the spirit realm. How would knowing this affect how you feel about your role in their deaths? Wouldn't that mean that in the end, you were merely an instrument in how they left—and not a deciding factor? What if, even though you pulled a trigger or threw a grenade, you didn't actually kill them—but merely put into play the circumstances that were already predetermined to allow them to reenter the spirit world?

Don't get me wrong. In no way am I trying to lessen the gravity of taking human life. I know that you may carry intense guilt and be judging yourself harder than anyone will ever know. But I just want you to think about it in larger, more cosmic terms in which you are less in control than you think you are and not as morally responsible as you might believe yourself to be.

Life and death are far bigger than we understand them to be. I'm not saying that guilt for your role in the war—which most soldiers carry to some degree, no matter how justified the war is—isn't valid. I'm just trying to offer another perspective where larger forces and plans and purposes may be at play, instead of our assumption that we human beings are the ultimate life force and that everything we do has immediate moral repercussions.

We value life because it is sacred. *Because we have no control over it.*

We fear death for the same reason.

And survivors live with intense reactions because in war they are suddenly immersed in both. There is a sense of control—and it is that assumption of control—weapon in your hands, the decision to use deadly force—that creates a strange mixture of guilt, power, and fear; often combined with thrills that teeter on the brink of sexual pleasure as the moment is lived in the vapor of undiluted life and pure death.

You feel the blood, guts, and brains on your skin and witness the complete mutilation of human bodies; you see the children used as explosive devices; touch buddies heaving their last breath; live in a state of near-death, ready to pounce, too exhausted to move, forcing yourself to go out on one more mission. In the midst of it all, you see life and death played out in nanosecond scenes—talking to a pal one moment, the next he's lying dead; closing eyes for just a moment of sleep, the next being thrown into the air as an explosion knocks your ears out. Living on the edge of existence in this world and life in the next—whatever afterlife you believe in—changes who you are. It sends your soul into fetal position or causes it to simply take flight.

Surviving is not just about escaping death. It's about *living through it.*

And every war survivor has lived through it.

Do you see why you would come out of it carrying little of who you were when you went in? It is not just a matter of training, skill, endurance, courage, and obeying orders. It is a matter of living in a place of soul-spirit that is somewhere between life here and life beyond. There is no room for who you were before. You've been stripped down to your mere soul-essence, and this is where you must start from when you return home.

What about the souls of those you've killed? Do you feel like they haunt you? Why do they haunt you? The result of death is always the same, but how you die is not. Consider, for a moment, who you are—your 'self'—your thoughts, feelings, your ability to think of yourself as a soul, your concept of yourself as a person—believe for a moment that this self cannot be killed. It continues to exist, with the same thoughts, perceptions, and consciousness after death.

So, one moment you are thinking about whether or not an insurgent is hiding in that building twenty yards ahead—the next you are suddenly without a body, seeing the scene from a different angle—and still wondering if that insurgent is up ahead. Except, you are dead. You don't feel any different. Are you dead? You look around. Your best buddy is crying. Your body is lying there, lifeless. Yes—no. It can't be. You are. Aren't you?

Some believe that souls have a hard time believing they are no longer in the body when death comes suddenly or violently. Almost as if the soul is in shock. Instead of moving on to the next realm, the soul lingers, unable to believe it has left the body.

My father, a Korean veteran, fought cancer for almost a year with as much gusto as any soldier, defying odds, and stubbornly refusing to give up hope. As his body literally drowned itself in fluid, he wrestled with his death for days. After he died, every night for six months he came to me in a dream, still ill, sitting in his wheel chair, emaciated, hairless, and frail. We'd talk; he'd ask me things and smile until the moment would come when I would realize something was wrong. He wasn't supposed to be there. I would then have to tell him that he had, in fact, died. The shock and disappointment on his face every night was the hardest part to bear. He just couldn't believe it. Sometimes he would start crying, realizing that he was no longer in his body. That he'd lost the fight. I'll never forget the look in his eyes.

The souls of the dead may visit the one who last saw them or has a connection to the moment when they left the body. If you see or feel the souls of those you've killed or those who have died, don't think that you are crazy. We know so little of the spirit realm. Your experience is real. Many soldiers feel that these souls are there to haunt them, to punish them, when, in reality, these souls often just want reassurance that their life mattered.

Don't be afraid to talk to the dead.

Consider this: if you were killed by an insurgent and back in the spirit world, do you think it would matter to you afterward who the person was who killed you? Would you be filled with revenge and hatred—or do you think, after death, souls return to a state of innocence, to a higher consciousness where greater visions of purpose and positive energy outweigh the events that took place on earth? Could it be possible that after death, evil no longer exists? That there is no hell? If that could be so, then the souls of those you have killed would not be interested in tormenting you—but instead, might want the connection that you offer to their last moment on earth.

Consider too, if you feel or see the souls of those who have died, that *your* soul may not be ready to let them go yet, either. Perhaps they are waiting for you to accept what happened, to acknowledge them, forgive you, and have you forgive yourself before they can find peace. There is compassion beyond the grave.

Whether or not you see or feel people who have died around you, when you are ready, find a place to be alone and offer those you have killed a measure of understanding that your actions ended their time on earth. Reassure them that their lives mattered—move beyond political beliefs and see them as someone's son, brother, husband, father, child. As much as you were fighting on one side and believing in your truths, they were fighting on their side and believing in theirs. Those who died and were not fighting, were trapped in between. In the end, you are both simply human beings caught in the times and circumstances of your era. Stand with them in the spiritual realm and cry. Yes, cry. You don't have to love them, or forgive them, or feel sorry for them. Just acknowledge that because they were human beings their lives mattered. Circumstances shaped how things played out; but you were the one who ended their earth-time and your soul has touched theirs. Acknowledge that. If you feel a need, ask for their acceptance.

If you have souls around you who you feel haven't crossed over or have issues keeping them from crossing over, consider asking someone who practices Shamanism to help them through the process. See http://www.shamanism.org in the list of resources at the end of this book.

Whatever you do, just be and feel whatever you feel right now. Wouldn't you think a soul who has moved on to the spirit realm has the capacity to be bigger and stronger and more deeply understanding of those who are still on earth? Realize that those you have killed may have no ill feelings at all towards you. They can see the bigger picture. Yes, you may have cost them time they assumed they would have with their loved ones, but in reality, it was simply their time.

Your time—to keep living—is now. The dead do not want you to waste your life devoted to them. They've moved on; they no doubt have other purposes to fulfill. It's the living who need your attention. And right now, you need it the most.

Beginning to Let Go

You will also be faced with the dead who killed people you cared about—the enemy and in some cases where "friendly fire" or suicide is involved, your fellow soldiers. Your anger is justified. Your loss is real and meaningful. Forgiveness can be a confusing word. For most people, it has come to mean not holding someone responsible for the pain they've caused. The 'forgive and forget' theory makes many people think that they don't have a right to be as angry as they are or that they need to deny the true depth of pain they feel.

Acceptance and letting go are more accurate terms for what traditionally is known as forgiveness. You don't have to 'forgive' anyone who has killed people you love and miss. You don't have to forgive insurgents or that damn kid you thought just needed help and then blew himself up and killed three of your buddies. What you will have to do, someday, is come to a point where you look behind the actions of that damn kid and realize that perhaps an insurgent was cutting the arms off his sisters until he agreed to do it.

You don't have to forgive. And you may never be forgiven. It will never be okay what happened to you or what you did to someone else. But eventually, if you open to it, you will journey to a place where a wider perspective of humanity—one that includes both yourself and your enemy—will give you the grace to stop judging and offer true acceptance.

Don't deny the anger you feel right now. It's part of the process of healing. It tells you something isn't acceptable, something is wrong. Anger means that on a deep level, your spirit knows that the soul has been violated—yours and someone else's.

I never imagined that I could feel the depth of rage that I did when I started hearing and writing news stories about war criminals and people who had done unthinkable, sadistic acts to people I had come to know and care about. The perpetrators stopped being human beings in my mind. They stopped being people at all. My heart felt a solid, black nothingness for them.

Part of my anger was coupled with the fact that I felt so powerless to change what had happened or to make anything better for those who had survived. I wanted revenge. I wanted to take those war criminals out, murder their grandkids before their eyes, plow them under with bulldozers, dig them up again as limbs ripped off, then set them all on fire. I wanted the war criminals to watch; to feel it all; to have their hearts gutted from the inside out as their precious loved ones died while they stood there helpless. In my mind, at the time, this would have been justice—their style. After all, these were things they had done. To people I loved.

I felt no guilt over this. In fact, I soon realized how easy killing someone could be. I could understand a bit better how people can torture and kill those they no longer value as equal human beings. What once seemed as a completely unthinkable act suddenly wasn't so far out of mind.

Of course, I didn't act on my desire. I realized that even if I had been able to pay them back, it still wouldn't have changed what they had done. The people they had killed would still be dead. The pain of the survivors would still be there.

It took me a long time to realize that my anger wasn't a righteous way of holding on to those who had died. It served no one. It simply kept me angry, bitter, sarcastic; cut off from truly living and stuck in a war that had ended years before—a war perpetuated in my heart by my refusal to let go.

In the end, I did let it go.

And so will you. You will find a way to let go of the illusion of having control and let go of the rage to make space in your spirit for the future.

No, it doesn't have to be today. It may take you awhile to get to that place. But for now, let the thought live in you.

Your soul is a precious thing. You may be mired down in such filth and grime that you can't even remember what it feels like to be clean and whole. The images in your body may be so overwhelming that you can't imagine how you will ever get over this. The idea that you will someday not feel guilty, or that you will be able to accept what happened, may seem absurd and impossible. You can swear on it.

I am here to tell you that underneath it all, you are a human being worthy of compassion, empathy, and love. You have the right to be enjoyed and to know that you bring joy to those around you. You are not a monster, no matter how dark the feelings may be. You are a soldier and a war survivor.

And you will recover.

Voices

BEFORE I WAS BORN

Tonight a siren sounds and fades to black.
The cold and callous night takes away
the strength of breathing vapors cast upon the track.

Somewhere a pain exists,
Somewhere a pain is felt and dealt,
there in that room or field,
blood runs more red than hate.

I have fought from days of first,
and fought from days to last,
my energy does tire from me,
but I have a day to recompense my wrath.

I poured out in days of old,
I poured out through the pain,
I managed to survive years of this,
yet, somehow I remain.

Wars have come and gone,
they all seem so the same,
some between a man or nation,
some no one particularly to blame,
the only truth that lies in them,
they were born and they were called by name.

I knew from the day I was born,
my time on earth was a war.
I didn't come to win a thing,
I only came to fight and nothing more.

My life a waste, some will say, and surely so,
yet, oh the things I have seen and places I did go.
Names, nations, faces,
languages and skills.
All the part of training me to be the man that kills.

So wonder why a man like me,
so humble and unrepaired,
could care or dare to say a word,
that hell has found a playful dance,
and the devil has combed his hair.

Yes, I pulled trigger, a thousand if not one,
I brought blood upon the ground,
from innocent feathers light,
I destroyed lives that I can count,
and they remind me in the night.

You see me now and think that I am not,
the person you have made of me,
that person long forgot.

The me inside of me,
that is where I live,
I pour my sweat and cry my tears,
I bleed for my disdain,
I know the things that I have done,
and all my works in vain.

Countries I traveled, places I did go,
Languages I have learned,
and yet, I have no place to grow.
Everywhere I set my foot,
I find a memory of hurt,
places where I cast my works
and places where my work was turned to dirt.

You can't know the things in me,
and you never will,
there is a part of me that is the most,
the part that dares to kiss then kill.
It isn't my desire to hurt nor my way,
I only strive to be the boy once I knew,
and turn from my horrid days.

I plead for mercy on an altar stone,

I pray for God to take away,
the record I have grown.
No one knows more than I,
the pain I have placed upon the race,
of nations not my own.
I only tried to do my best,
and do the things I was told.
I did my best and damned I am,
for thinking I was in the right.
I did my best and I survived the rest,
and took my pennies in gold,
awards upon my chest,
wounds in my soul,
I gave it all that I could give,
and some how the master I had become,
the one that walked the world unknown,
the one with power to destroy,
I had become the simple toy,
the man they turned back to be a boy.

—Lonnie D. Story, U.S. Army Special Forces[4]

What's Running Through My Mind Now…

4

Sacred Space

✦

War survivors often find that the rush of activity at homecoming masks their spirit's need for space. There is a natural spiritual and emotional disconnect between the battlefield and home life. This gap is what demands space—living and breathing space that will let your body and spirit re-orient. In the celebration of reuniting with loved ones, rediscovering home and community and addressing pressing business and financial matters, survivors can get caught up in a false sense of well-being. The busyness feels good because it is a distraction and offers a sense of return to normal life, but in reality, it does not reconnect you.

Unfortunately, our society is uncomfortable with space and stillness. We are uncomfortable with the void space creates because we do not know how to live in our souls. Instead, we fill our lives up with constant sound, noise, and conversation. And yet, our spirits crave stillness and attention. Our thoughts want to be examined, beliefs questioned, feelings sorted out, future imagined.

You need to pull back from the rush of home life and *create a sacred space* for yourself, for rest, and for your wounds. By creating a sacred space around your spirit, a space that is intended just to be as it is—without pressure to heal, to change, to recover, to do anything—you create a place within that gives your spirit a chance to breathe. A chance to let your spirit catch up with your body.

Life at home can, and most often will, come crashing in on you—with complete disregard for your inner wounds and the deep rest your body needs. Unless you make a conscious effort to create this space, the busyness of daily routines will shove your spirit aside.

I'm not saying that you should just sit around and do nothing all day, every day. Men in particular find physical activity and movement an essential part of their healing process. What I'm talking about is not letting the *distraction* of busyness and activity mask the rest and space your soul needs to recover.

You need space. To be. To exist. To sit still and do nothing. Physically and spiritually. Most returning soldiers do not have the chance to take time for themselves when they get home. Too much is going on. Too much needs to be addressed. Bills have to be paid and businesses have to be run. Spouses need relief and kids need attention.

So, how can you create sacred space?

First of all, don't get distracted by the term. Sacred space is an *attitude*. It's an awareness. It's recognizing that in the midst of everything you have to do and all the social demands on you, you still need a place to retreat and shut out all the noise.

It means giving yourself *permission* to have the time and space you need not to do anything. Sacred space gives you a place where no one, but you, is allowed to go. The inner rest you need is built on the attitude that *it's okay just to be who you are and not have to do or change or heal or fix anything.* Men are generally better at taking time for themselves than women. Men retreat when they need time alone.

While there are incredible demands on every returning soldier, women in particular are prone to putting their own need for rest on the back burner while they take care of everyone else. Women veterans may also feel a more acute sense of guilt about being away from children, spouses, and jobs that keeps them driving themselves to give more than they can really afford. As a woman, it takes courage to find time for yourself (and to give it to yourself) by telling others that you need it. Yet, you simply can't expect yourself to return from your tour and have the energy to be the mom, spouse, partner, daughter, sister, employee, and friend that everyone will want you to be. Let's face it, people love you. They want to be with you, and they take comfort in seeing you return to a non-soldier role. What they may not see is that you need time for recovery, for renewal, and that you may not have the emotional stamina to give much at all. It will take a lot of patience and commitment to yourself to explain to others that you simply need time. Yet, it's imperative that you put your healing first.

It can also be particularly uncomfortable as a woman to know that others do not understand you. While this also bothers men, we women tend to base a lot of our self-worth on how accepted we are by others. When people don't understand us, or make us feel selfish for the choices we make, it hurts, and we start to question ourselves. Let me tell you something I've learned as a writer: people's *response* to you doesn't change who you are. Everyone will have their own response based on their own experiences, personality, ideas, etc. You are who you are. And you are the only one who can validate yourself. So, let people not understand or judge you—it can't change who you really are. Don't let anyone stop you from making decisions that move your toward healing.

Many of us have grown up making sure all our waking hours are filled with activity and noise. The idea of space can be a little unsettling. Don't be afraid of the quiet. Don't be afraid that the memories will overtake you. Quiet is not the enemy. The enemy is being afraid to sit with the memories. If the quiet is too quiet and you find it hurts too much, then make space and involve activity.

You don't have to focus on your wounds in your sacred space, either. This isn't a therapy session. Focus on life, on what is going right for you, on the things that interest you. Begin to dream a little. Think bigger. Start remembering how powerful (in a good way) you really are in this world. Realize that *you are not your wounds*. This is especially important if you have physical or mental wounds that are labeled with a diagnosis. *You are not your wounds.* You are a whole person who happens to be wounded. You may need to redesign your identify, but for now, don't focus on how wounded you are. Give yourself permission to not think about it for awhile. Let your space be your time for breathing, for renewal, for pause, for taking a nap.

Remember that healing is a *process*. You want to be better within weeks after coming home. When this doesn't happen, society labels survivors as unstable or writes them off as people who just 'couldn't get over the war.' As if they are weaker than others. According to the National Coalition of Homeless Veterans, over two-hundred thousand veterans are homeless on any given night. Only forty-seven percent of those are Vietnam veterans[5]. Iraq and Afghanistan vets are quickly joining those numbers. How do veterans become homeless? Often because their war trauma or PTSD makes getting or holding a job next to impossible, then bills mount up, money runs out, the VA takes too long, and all of a sudden there's no place to call home. There are also countless other veterans we, as a society, disregard simply because we do not know how, and do not want, to acknowledge the reality of what war does to the soul.

Survivors feel this pressure. If healing does not come quick enough, it's easy to despair and start second-guessing yourself. Even though you *know* war will be a part of who you are forever.

Your survivor instincts on this are right. It's our society that's wrong.

As much as survivors need sacred space, at the same time they must not be ignored. There is a huge difference. Sacred space is acknowledged. It is warm, accepting, open space that creates a buffer around your spirit and mind and gives you the freedom to ask questions, to explore beliefs, to let whatever you are, and wherever you are in relation to healing simply *be enough* right now. It is an acceptance that acknowledges your woundedness and still leaves you feeling validated and respected.

When loving families and caring communities give it, you sense you belong and that you matter. *It tells you that you are essentially okay no matter how messed up you think you are.* It lets you know that there are loving people who are standing ready to give you whatever you need to move toward wholeness. There is an absence of expectations, judgment, or pressures. There are no insinuations that you should or shouldn't be feeling or thinking a certain way, no effort to control your emotions, responses or beliefs, no assertions that you are or are not healing fast enough, that life should or should not be the way it is right now.

At the same time, accepting how you feel for the moment also means accepting help. If you feel intense violence or anger and you think you may hurt yourself or someone else, you need to accept the fact that you need to get help. Immediately. If you are having violent thoughts towards people around you, you need to prevent something tragic from happening.

Families also need to understand that accepting a survivor's pain means that you recognize that that pain may cloud his or her judgment, and you may need to step in and call for help if you feel unsafe or are worried for your own or your survivor's safety. It's hard to actually step out and take action, because our mind keeps trying to deny that a situation is as bad or as dangerous as it seems—but getting help is crucial and may mean the difference between life and death. It's better to seek help and find out it wasn't needed, then to not get help and realize later that you could have done something. If you sense in your gut, or there is a little voice in the back of your head warning you, do not ignore it. Call someone right now and get help. Your intuition and the feeling in your body are right. Don't let reason or your desire to not want to face what it means if your intuition is right, talk you into ignoring warning sensations.

Sacred space is needed for healing, but what does sacred space look like in reality?

For the survivor, it is a self-created place inside—some imagine it to be a place around the heart or spirit—a place where there is no pressure, where you are safe—as safe as you can be right now—and where everything you are, right now, is perfectly okay and free to be (again, if you are feeling violent or intense anger, you do need to get help immediately).

It is also an effort to take actual time for yourself—whether it's fifteen minutes, an hour a day, an entire week, or more—whatever time you can carve out to just be free. No pressures to relate, to hide your reactions, to wear the mask. It's time for you to grieve and mourn and begin to process everything that you have been through. It gives you a place to create distance among what you are experiencing inside, where you are living, and the world you have to relate to now. It also gives you a chance to start to see the joy and satisfaction that life still has for you.

Communities and employers give sacred space by not ignoring survivors or assuming that if they look fine and say they're fine, they are. Communities can recognize that survivors will need years to recover and can set up assistance and outreach programs to fill in the gap for military families. It can be as simple as publicly discussing what war does to the soul.

Communities can also create sacred space around a survivor by showing profound respect. This needs to go beyond the welcome home parties and parades. Communities should create policies that assist, define, and honor war survivors in public and private ways. Religious groups and employers can sponsor a survivor and his or her family's vacation. Or sponsor a babysitter for one night a week for several months.

For families, creating sacred space begins with communicating. With telling your survivor that you are there for them, that you can't imagine what they are going through. It's a reassurance that you love the survivor anyway, that they are acceptable, and the assurance that what they are feeling, or not feeling, is normal for what they have lived through. It is recognizing that the survivor is wounded and not pressuring him or her to heal, change, or recover. It's seeking help when you feel unsure.

It is not ignoring or failing to talk about things. It takes courage on the loving family's part to be the first to start the conversation—to sit down and outright say that you do not know or understand what the survivor has been through, but that you accept them wholly as they are, and that you know they need space to be. It's not commenting on how the survivor is dealing with things, but letting them know that it's okay for them to deal with the war on their own terms—as long as those terms aren't dangerous or destructive to you, the survivor, or family.

Creating sacred space requires continued sacrifice. It does. And as hard is it is for spouses and families exhausted from solely supporting the family, it's important to remember that the war doesn't end when a survivor comes home.

Understandably, when a survivor returns is often when spouses and families want nothing more than to collapse in the survivor's caring arms and let him or her help handle life for a while. Spouses and families also need a break and need sacred space. *But they cannot get it solely from the survivor.*

This is a time when spouses and families must draw on their tenacious strength, rely on their newfound independence, and gather support from extended family and close friends. Families can form partnerships—a shared vision of handling the household responsibilities together and a commitment to moving toward healing and reconnection. The survivor can meet certain needs and definitely needs to be needed—but they cannot be expected to pick up the reigns alone.

The danger after war lies when spouses and families take on the attitude that now that the survivor is back, everything is back to normal, and there is no longer any need to sacrifice. It is unrealistic to assume that a survivor will be able to jump right back in to handling family and life responsibilities as if nothing traumatic has happened to them.

As a spouse or partner, it's hard when you are already depleted to continue to give and be the strong one. But it's necessary. Your survivor is wounded. No matter what your survivor says, he or she is not "okay." Survivors need your nurturing, your strength, and the freedom that comes from knowing you are there and that you can handle things for and with them. Survivors don't want to burden you more—and they don't want to hurt you with their burdens.

You may be the only one in the survivor's life who has the ability to see things as they are. You may be the only one who has the perspective to see that what he or she needs most is space, acceptance, nurturing, and rest.

But, what about me? Spouses often ask. As a spouse or partner, you've been handling the fear and stress of worrying about your soldier, keeping the family going with added financial burdens, the exhausting stress of waking up alone every morning, caring for the kids, and having to do every single thing on your own. You've also suffered. You also need sacred space.

Survivors need to realize that partners and spouses need sacred space and they have a deep need for you to understand and know what it was like for him/her while you were gone. Communication is hard when you're exhausted. If you aren't able to sit down and talk about it, e-mail each other. Explain from your heart what life was like for you, what you feared most, what kept you going. Then give each other time to read, to let it sink in, and respond.

Remember, during all of this, that you are both *exhausted*. Exhausted people are short on patience, say things they regret, and don't have the energy to communicate well. Give yourself this understanding, some grace to realize that neither one of you is at your best or even your 'normal' self. This is a good time to realize how valuable a therapist or counselor can be to help you communicate what you really mean and not what exhaustion has you saying.

Your entire family needs space where no one may enter. It may take asking for help and for people to support you to get this space. Be a warrior in your vigilance to create sacred space in your family. This space is what is going to allow healing to occur. *This is the place where healing will occur.*

The danger in sacred space is the tendency to confuse it with isolation. Sacred space feels like a welcome relief—isolation feels empty and scary. Sacred space is acknowledged, recognized, and respected. Isolation happens when people are ignored, remain silent, and do not accept the reality of war.

So, talk about what the war has taken from each of you and how it's also made you stronger. Begin to accept that the future will not be like the past, and start to imagine what a future of wholeness might look like. Spend time focusing on the gifts in life you have *right now*, and appreciate the little things. When you start to see nothing but lack and needs and impossibilities—stop. Shift your focus to today and to this moment. Look around you—most likely you'll discover that, yes, indeed, you do have everything you need right now. Tomorrow may be unsure, but right now is all you have anyway.

Life is precariously precious. If anyone knows that now, you do. Look at yourself through the vast eyes of the Universe. Schedule time to spend alone, as a couple and a family. And remember it's okay to play. People going through grief and loss often feel guilty if moments of bright humor and sunlight come flooding in—but it's okay to be happy even during loss.

It's okay to be whatever you are in your sacred space.

Voices

MIA

Missing in Action
doesn't mean just not
coming back from the green.

So many nights you sit across the room from me
and you are here—not here.
It and *they* are with me, in you.
It is there in your eyes
in your stare;
the green, tentacled canopy
spreading from your eyes to your heart,
like orchids slowly dying in greasy silver rain,
clutching your soul in twisted dark.

You are here—not here.
It is in you, *they* are all with you,
in you
and so many nights there is
no room for me.

And I, so desperately, need holding
that you can't give
that I boil an egg to clutch in my hand,
just for some kind of soft warmth touching me.

—Remy Benoit
from *warm, glowing woman*[6]

What's Running Through My Mind Now…

5

Loss

✦

"I just don't understand. It all seems so meaningless. I watched three of my best friends die. Now I'm back and I don't know why I feel so empty. I miss those guys. A lot."

"I don't know why I am alive. I've killed children, for god's sake! I should have died a thousand times. Why the hell am I still here?"

"I'm angry. I mean fuck'n angry. Sometimes I look at someone doing something stupid and I just want to put my hands around their neck and strangle them. You think I'll go to hell? I mean, killing just got so easy, you know? Sometimes I think there's something really fucked up in me. I mean, a good person wouldn't feel like this, would they?"

War steals. And what it takes most profoundly from us is *relationship.* Our relationship to ourselves, our past, our present, our future, our loved ones, our communities, our work, our faith, our worldview, and our purpose in life. Loving families face the loss of relationship to the survivor, and the loss of aspects of the survivor that they cherished and trusted. Families also face the loss of their expectations for what the future will be like.

Soldiers return home saturated in death. Death is the loss of life as we know it.

While coming home is an event to be celebrated, it's in the ensuing months and years ahead when the tidal wave of just how much a survivor has lost will come crashing in. The battlefield's focus on survival and on living in the moment shields survivors from the full impact. The sudden change to life back home gives the mind and body a chance to begin to make a self-assessment, tallying just how much damage has been done. For some, the process of identifying their losses may come slowly. Others may feel the full impact immediately.

Regardless of how the level of loss is revealed to the consciousness, survivors are people facing intense grief. Loved ones also face grief for what war has taken from their survivor and from their life with the survivor.

It's okay to feel sad.

Permission to Grieve, Sir!

Our society's propensity for assuming that survivors return home from war and within twenty-four to forty-eight hours simply get on with life and that they should be jubilant to be alive and celebrating life is a stark reminder of how deeply our culture denies the realities of war.

Survivors are grieving, not just their own loss, but for friends and comrades who have died or been permanently injured, for people they have killed, and for the myriad of losses they have accumulated in their time deployed.

As a survivor, you need time to grieve. Our society will not give it to you. This is part of the sacred space you must create and give to yourself—an acceptance that you need to grieve, that *it is only natural that you are sad and experiencing sensations of loss, anger, and uncertainty.*

The act of killing, and living, inside a world of death causes a loss of relation with the self. Killing causes a loss of relation with other human beings, and death breaks relation with friends and comrades. Death and violence create questions that we cannot answer. These questions are what break our relation to life as we know it and to our worldview.

War creates the most profound loss known to humanity: our faith in ourselves as beings created with purpose. We lose bearing on our humanity and hold on to what we can, while questions eat away—until we feel there is nothing left.

From the moment you are first exposed to war you are in a state of being disassembled. Only after war will life move to put the pieces back together in a new form. There may be pieces missing that will never come back, jagged holes in memory, feelings, what you wanted in life. Survivors and loved ones begin the healing process by accepting that the past is gone, that the present exists, and that each moment begins a future that can offer you a new definition of wholeness and purpose. That future begins with recognizing the present for what it is.

The losses you feel are real. And they must be honored. *It's okay to grieve and to grieve for a long time.*

Forget the admonition to get over it quickly. Forget the cultural pressure to deny pain and wear a mask. This is *your life* we are talking about. *Your life.* You deserve to grieve and honor what you have lost and what you have sacrificed. Your children deserve a parent who takes his or her pain seriously enough to deal with it in a healthy way—in a human way. The hardest part may be not finding the support to allow yourself the opportunity to do this. That's where loved ones must fill in the gap and communities should take meaningful action.

Ultimately, you must recognize that you are a person in pain and that anyone who expects anything different than that simply isn't dealing with reality. Your losses are real.

Grieving the Loss of Boundaries

Soldiers are trained to tap into a primal instinct that allows them to kill while at the same time they are disciplined to keep that urge under control. Most soldiers do. However, the reality is that killing can become so easy, and situations so complex, that soldiers may commit or be ordered to commit atrocities and acts of torture. Throughout history, soldiers have always done this. It's just that the American public has not had to face this part of the reality of war until incidents in My Lai, Vietnam, and more recently the 2004 torture accounts at Abu Ghraib, Iraq, came to light.

Soldiers are not murderers. They are people appointed to kill for society. You cannot expect people to kill and not fall prey to losing boundaries. Killing another human being *is* the loss of all boundaries. What we dispute is how we kill and how long it takes the other to die. Many survivors silently carry these secret realities and the tremendous guilt that goes with them—whether from having committed, witnessed, or having found themselves unable to prevent them. Because society is not willing to accept its own humanity, we perpetuate the myth that we are always the good guy and our enemies are always inherently evil. This creates a gap in consciousness where our soldiers are forced to keep the shocking realities of war a secret, and our society is not allowed to shoulder the full burden of war with them.

It's human nature to want to be the "good guys" in war—every army believes its cause is just. As Americans, we want to treat our enemies humanely, hold on to moral standards of compassion, empathy, and fairness. And most of our troops do. However, many troops feel deep guilt that this wasn't their reality on the battlefield. What really happens in war and what we want to believe happens in war are often two different things.

Should soldiers just kill identifiable enemies? In an ideal war, yes. Do soldiers kill just identifiable enemies? No. They kill whoever they have to and sometimes whoever just happens to be there. That's war.

War does not operate under the same moral compass as civilian life. What you are asked to do in war is what you do; what you have to do in war is what you do. When it conflicts with your own beliefs about the sanctity of life is when you face the true reality of war.

Survivors come home facing an internal world that knows what war really is and an external world that does not. The difference between the two creates a conflict that leaves a survivor questioning his own humanity and so trapped inside the guilt that sometimes they feel there is little choice but to self-destruct.

If you have committed atrocities, tortured teenagers, raped, killed children, dug mass graves, or other things you can't put into words and been forced to cover it up—you are not alone. And you should not have to shoulder that human burden alone. The guilt you feel may be overwhelming and you may feel dirty or even unworthy to live. Unfortunately, no one wants to hear that from you. Our society would like to believe the news reports that only a handful of soldiers are responsible for atrocities—it's easier for us to blame a few "bad" soldiers then to understand that what we call 'atrocities' are often an inherent part of war.

Whatever you have done in war, you need to understand that you were in an environment that could not be controlled, operating under the command of individuals who were also in the same situation. You may have been in a frame of mind where you made decisions that should not have been made. No doubt, you faced orders that made no sense and decisions made by people who may not have understood the situation in your area.

There were forces at work that you did not have control over. One of those forces may have been yourself. You may believe that you are not able to justify your actions, but please remember as you are judging yourself that war is something far greater than you. What you did in war is part of what you have lost.

Mourning the Dead

Survivors need to mourn the dead. Don't bury the grief you sense in your chest, thinking that it shouldn't affect you this much. It's not something you leave behind. Your spirit needs to mourn the people you have lost and the people you have killed.

Your friends—the people who fought alongside you, defended you, went through hell with you, then died or were permanently injured—they meant something. They were special. They *are* special and will be for the rest of your life. Losses can pile up so high that you may be numb right now. That's okay. Someday you will find a way to honor them.

Is it strange to mourn the people you have killed? Not at all. Taken out of the battlefield context, all lives are equal. All souls are equal. And even those who are "evil" in earthly action have souls that return to an afterlife where evil does not exist. When you mourn all the lives lost in war, it reflects your own humanity and the eternal loss that human beings suffer in war. Do not deny yourself the grief you feel as a human being who has been deeply touched by war.

What if you don't feel sad? What if you don't feel guilty? What if you don't feel anything at all? Is there something wrong with you? No. War wraps you in layer after layer of emotions, reactions, and sensation. Our survival core—the deepest parts of our spirit—reacts in whatever way it needs to in order to survive. Going numb is normal, not feeling anything is normal. Don't let the absence of feeling convince you that you aren't a caring being or that you aren't capable of love.

Feelings will surface when your soul is ready for them. It may take a long time or it may happen suddenly. When they do come, allow yourself to experience them. Remember that your thoughts and feelings are part of you, but *they are not who you are* and they are not facts. They are reactions that allow your spirit to process life and experience the fullness of what it means to be human.

The Grieving Process

Grieving is a process. It takes time and shows up differently in everyone. Generally, there are five stages of grief, as outlined by Elisabeth Kubler-Ross in her 1969 classic *On Death and Dying*. Not everyone experiences all of these; and they don't happen in any particular order. You can cycle through them, feel just one the most, and take months to years to experience them.

They are:

1. **Denial.** This can include feeling numb and feeling nothing at all, to complete disbelief. You may believe that you are fine, that you're not grieving, and get annoyed when people suggest that you may be grieving.
2. **Anger.** Anger can come in refusing to accept what happened, feeling rage, disappointment, betrayal; and feeling anger at yourself, at others, and at the person who died.
3. **Bargaining.** This is where you're willing to trade anything to change what happened. If only you could go back and do something differently.
4. **Depression.** Feeling sad, loss of energy, not interested in talking about the war or the people lost, feeling trapped in guilt, life doesn't seem worth living, and feeling nothing at all about anything.
5. **Acceptance.** This comes when you begin to know that you can go on, that it's okay to be happy without the people who've died, and that by living your life fully you honor those who are gone.[7]

Your losses are numerous after war. Grief isn't just for those who've died or been injured. You can grieve time gone from family, important family events you missed, physical wounds, lost relationships, possessions that were sold when you were absent, missing a key promotion at work, and the loneliness of being misunderstood. And yes, you may even miss the war.

The Family's Grief

War causes intense loss in survivors; the battlefield death of friends and enemies, the sense of fragmenting—only a survivor can carry these. *But everything else that war does to a survivor is part of what loved ones lose in war.*

Loved ones lose a precious recognition in the survivor—they lose knowing the survivor fully and aspects of them that they cherished and counted on. They also lose the expectations they had of what the future will be like. From changes in sex life to finances, dealing with physical war injuries, missed family events, to even just being able to anticipate what the survivor will do next—loved ones lose relationship with the survivor.

As a survivor, you need to realize that your partner, children, parents and family are going through their own sense of loss. They've dealt with incredible fear, tension, loneliness, uncertainty, physical exhaustion from taking care of kids, work, dealing with finances, carrying worry alone, and trying to be brave and smile at everyone who asks them how they're doing—when in truth, they often felt like they were dying inside. It's amazing how alone a partner can feel just from the fact that they know everything that happened in the household during the deployment and the survivor doesn't. Memories that should have been made together, but weren't, are some of the loneliest memories there are. Families have also had to deal with the unsupportive things people have said against the war and their own conflicting mix of how they felt about the war with their support of you.

Life has changed in your absence, and for women in particular that's one of the hardest things to deal with. Women are generally sensitive to the subtle changes in a relationship that come from not being together. As women, we depend on physical nearness of loved ones to really know how they are doing, to build friendship, to express love. All our fears, insecurities, and worst imaginings can take over when we can't actually be with someone we're worried about. You can be sure that for a loving spouse left behind, every moment when you were gone, part of them felt like it was ripped out and missing. For me, when Sasha would go out on dangerous reporting assignments, I would have rather risked physical danger myself just to know how he was and be there if something happened than stay behind. You can go crazy waiting, not knowing.

A hidden cost of war is the multiple, layered losses that families experience during and after war. Even when the survivor comes back alive and well, families need to grieve. You can be caught off guard by feelings of sadness and loss when you assume that just because a survivor comes back alive, everything should be magically okay again. The reality is that when the pressure is off, the body and spirit start processing all the emotions that have been pent up and held for so long. It can be confusing when you believe you should be happy, but experience unexplained episodes of sadness and crying. It's okay. Your body and spirit are moving through a time of transition. It's okay to realize how much you have been carrying, how stressed you have been, how alone you have felt. The whole family is fragile and incredibly strong—it's okay if you need help supporting each other.

One of our society's most painful faults is our inability to openly grieve. It seems we lost this somewhere along the way—our tough, independent spirit and an influx of mixed cultures has created a huge void when it comes to truly mourning loss of human life. We expect people who have a loved one die to heal quickly. Anyone who experiences the true time—two to ten years or more—that it takes to mourn and make a new sense of wholeness soon learns to keep their grief a secret. Just look at employer's policies of granting one to two days off for immediate family funerals. We expect people to lose a wife one day and within three days be back at work. Are we insane?

Consider this parable: Jack went to work one morning, and during the day his wife called to tell him that his brother had been killed in a car accident. Two weeks later his best childhood friend died from a heart attack. Six weeks later, his colleague he had worked with for nine years died in a boating accident. Four months later his sister died when her husband shot her. A week after that Jack was in a near fatal car crash. Two weeks later his youngest son had an acute asthma attack and was placed in intensive care. Four weeks later his wife was raped in the parking lot at the mall. Six weeks later his dad died from cancer.

Fiction, right? I mean, this couldn't possibly happen to one person! And yet, survivors and families experience a level of multiple traumatic losses *just as intense* as this and we fail to recognize it. This won't change unless we begin to speak out and help communities understand the actual impact of war's trauma in ways they can identify with. As long as the losses of war remain secret, no one will know. And how can we expect someone to show true empathy unless they do know?

It's okay to be grieving and to let people know that you are. Talk about it, let other people have a chance to understand, and be able to offer their support.

Remember, grieving takes time. It takes a sense of sacred space around your spirit that allows you to be gentle with yourself. It takes recognition that you and your family are experiencing a loss, and an allowance to be soft with each other.

It means not expecting each other to be your best; and having deep compassion for what the other is going through—even though you can't fully understand it.

It also takes vision—the ability to trust that what the present is now—full of anger and confusion and incredible sadness and fear—is not what the future will be. Hold on to a vision of a future full of wholeness. It does exist. It will for you.

Voices

The Child Death

Daddy had gone to heaven
On an IED.

I—E—D.
Like the letters on an eye chart
At the doctor's office.

How could letters send her Daddy to heaven?

Mommy said he was on a road
And hit an IED
And went to heaven.

Driving to the mall
She felt cold
Worried
Afraid

What if Mommy hit an IED?

—John Cory[8]

What's Running Through My Mind Now…

6
PTSD

✦

Post Traumatic Stress Disorder (PTSD) is one of the only post-war factors the public is fairly willing to discuss. Soldiers are evaluated for and debriefed on it and most military families are somewhat familiar with the concept. However, because we have come to associate PTSD with having been "affected" by the war, we assume that it is the *only* indicator of how well you're handling "the war." This is a huge mistake.

When survivors do *not* experience PTSD, we easily assume that the war did not impact them as deeply as it actually has. You don't have to have PTSD to be wounded from your war experiences.

And if you don't have PTSD, do not assume that you have nothing to heal or from which to recover. Your experience of war may actually be rooted deeper than those who openly display PTSD symptoms.

The Bosnian survivors I know and love carry their war trauma with them all the time. Most of the time, though, you'd never know it. They laugh, interact, joke, have fun, party, play, love, share friendship, and work hard. They also hide from thunder, jump at loud noises, tear up when a painful memory arrives, comment on the war throughout their everyday activities, feel mixed shame and fear, and find it hard to trust in general because everything they knew was destroyed by people they once believed in. Life has simply gone on; they have simply continued to live. Some know how and why, many never will.

While PTSD is common in war populations, any survivor can tell you that it is not an indicator of whether or not you've escaped war's impact.

Did you know that as of spring 2008, the Veterans Affairs Department estimates that only six to twenty percent of Iraq and Afghanistan veterans will develop PTSD?

For those unfamiliar with it, PTSD is a diagnosis for lingering physical and emotional reactions to trauma that interfere in daily life and relationships. It's characterized by frequently re-living the event (flashbacks and nightmares); avoidance (trying to avoid anything that triggers the memory); numbness (not feeling or distancing by not experiencing loving feelings toward family and friends) and a constant state of being keyed up or on edge (startling easy, excessive emotion/angry reactions to minor events, perceived danger, being over-protective).

The Veteran's Affairs Department has a National Center for PTSD where you can find fact sheets and practical data on PTSD, common symptoms, and treatment options. Access it at http://www.ncptsd.va.gov.

Healthcare providers have classified PTSD as a disorder. But it's not a 'disorder' in the sense that there is something flawed or weak in you if you experience it. PTSD is a *lingering reaction* to intense trauma and life-threatening events. War can be a constant state of life-threatening trauma. The symptoms and existence of PTSD are real, and many survivors will experience it. If you have it, you are not insane or crazy, even though PTSD may cause you to act and react in ways that seem inappropriate for your current circumstances. PTSD needs to be treated, just as much as a physical wound would, and there is no shame in getting help.

The danger of PTSD for a society lies in using it as the *only* indicator of war trauma. By labeling PTSD and focusing on it as the only "publicly recognized" response to trauma, we minimize the full spectrum of how war impacts the soul.

Because most survivors and their families are on the lookout for PTSD symptoms they may assume that PTSD is the only determination for how well a survivor is coping. Do not assume that if your survivor does not have PTSD symptoms that he or she has healed, that they are "getting on with life", or that the war is over for them. Do not assume, too, that if you don't have PTSD, you aren't entitled to talk about how the war has affected you and the memories you carry inside.

PTSD is a prolonged reaction to trauma, but *all trauma survivors have a reaction.*

Many war survivors recover naturally as time passes and yet the war will never be far from them. It's a disservice to our survivors when we only look for PTSD and do not realize that war permeates every aspect of the soul and that each survivor is profoundly impacted regardless of how the effects show up in their lives.

Every war survivor has suffered from war. Every survivor has memories, nightmares, flashbacks, triggers (things that bring back intense feelings and reactions to experiences), fears, uncertainties, and deep losses. Every survivor deals with these responses in his or her own way. The war may show up in different areas of your life at different times. It may happen now or in ten years, but it will show up. Do not use PTSD as the only indicator for how the war has impacted you.

Sexual Trauma in War

An increasingly common trauma far less talked about is military sexual trauma—which is experiencing sexual assault or harassment while you are in the military. This is not just a women's problem. In fact, the VA reports that fifty-five percent of women and thirty-eight percent of men in the military have experienced military sexual harassment[9]. While military sexual trauma is more common in women, *over half of all veterans with military sexual trauma are men.*

War has historically seen an increase in sexual assault and rape incidents for both military and war-zone populations. It's become more publicly recognized in war-zone civilian populations (mass gang rapes were widely reported during the Bosnian war and rape has traditionally been a way to violate an enemy population), but rarely do we hear about sexual assault among our own soldiers.

If you have experienced a sexual violation during war that has left you 'just not feeling the same' since, please know that *you are not alone.* Most victims of military sexual trauma will never report it. Whether or not you call it rape doesn't matter. What happened to you wasn't right and it wasn't your fault; and no, you couldn't have prevented or stopped it. Rape is always an issue of power, not sex. Unfortunately, rape in war happens too often as people deal with overwhelming feelings of god-like power, lowered inhibitions, excessive anger, lack of usual sexual release and the devaluation of human life—sexual force is often used with little outward consequence to the perpetrator. But the consequences to the victim can be life-changing.

If this has happened to you, you may develop PTSD from this alone, but be too embarrassed or humiliated to tell anyone why. This may be the hardest part of your war experience to deal with, and one that strangles you in secrecy, shame, and embarrassment. After all, with fellow survivors coming back with missing limbs and mental shock, how can having been sexually violated compare to that? No one would believe you, would they? What would loved ones think? Soldiers are supposed to be tough; how could you ever admit that you weren't strong enough to keep someone from forcing sex on you? Yet, for you, what happened has become your war. A war that no one will ever know anything about.

Please stop. Stop and take a deep breath. Forget the fact that it was a war environment for a moment and realize that no matter where it happens, when, or to whom, being sexually violated leaves a person feeling powerless, doubtful of themselves, uncertain, unable to believe it really happened, and feeling very, very small inside.

Why? Because sexual assault is about taking away your power. Sex is our most intimate and most powerful interaction with another human being. And when someone overpowers us physically and enters our bodies without our consent, we are deeply ashamed and shocked at how powerless we were.

Sexual violence injures the soul. The shame, humiliation, loss of control, and shaken self-esteem affect both men and women even though each gender experiences them differently because of what we are conditioned to believe about our masculine or feminine roles in life.

Sexual violation impacts our self-image, sexuality, and our future, safe sexual experiences. The overwhelming sense of vulnerability and shame can lead to suicidal thoughts and actions.

For war survivors who have been violated by one of their own, the confusion and uncertainty, not to mention potential repercussions to your military career or even survival, lead most victims to never tell anyone. Keeping your mouth shut may be the only way to survive and get back home. But once you are home, please realize that if this has happened to you, you have been affected and it's not just going to go away. It takes feeling safe to get yourself to the point where you can admit to someone that it happened. And for a lot of people, finding someone safe seems almost impossible.

If you tell no one else in your life, please call the National Sexual Assault Hotline at 1-800-656-4673 or visit them online for an anonymous chat at http://www.rainn.org. You can remain anonymous, and at least you will be able to talk with someone who deals with this trauma every day and can start to give you the resources you need to find healing. The VA also reports that it has counselors at every hospital trained to assist veterans with this issue. You can also visit http://www.ncptsd.va.gov, search for "military sexual trauma"—and a number of fact sheets will come up where you can learn additional information.

Remember, what happened to you was a crime, not just a misfortune of war. The person who assaulted you did not have the right to do this to you under any circumstances.

One of the hardest parts about having been sexually traumatized can be sharing that information with a spouse or partner. It's normal to worry about how they will accept you once they know what has happened; and to wonder how it will impact your intimate life together. Even though this trauma may loom large before your eyes, your partner loves you for who you are—not just your ability to have sex. You may find far more love and acceptance than you imagine. You are still attractive, beautiful, desirable, virile, and your partner still longs to experience sexual intimacy with you. You may struggle with feeling that you are not worth loving which is one of the ways sexual violation diminishes your own sense of power. But feelings are not facts. You are a human being worth being loved, enjoyed, and you deserve to experience sexual intimacy in a safe and caring relationship.

Partners of sexual assault survivors may feel a sense of rage, powerlessness, guilt for not having been able to protect your loved one, and a natural reaction to want to get even with the person who has hurt the person you love. Counseling individually and as a couple can be a safe place to express what you are feeling. You can also call the Sexual Assault Hotline—it's not just for survivors; they can assist family and friends.

Remember, as long as you don't tell your partner what happened, he or she will have no way of knowing what you are feeling, worried about, remembering, or associating with your current sex life. You may have no desire to have sex because of the trauma, but how will your partner know that? If you don't share, he or she may assume that they are no longer desirable and that you've lost interest. They may easily blame themselves or you. Don't lose your relationship because you are too ashamed to share what happened. Seek a counselor who can help you decide how to share this information. Don't shut out what may be the only true source of love and support in your life. Loving partners can be incredibly patient when it comes to sex and trauma, but you have to give them the chance to understand what you are going through.

If you have been sexually traumatized, it may seem that that experience now defines who you are. Shame, guilt, self-blame, denial, rage, depression, lack of self-worth, fear of being intimate again, aversion to being touched or approached without warning, doubts about whether or not you are still desirable, or if having been raped effects your sexual orientation (it doesn't) are all normal reactions. Just remember the trauma is real and intimate, but you are not defined by what has happened to you. You are a whole person who has experienced vulnerability and powerlessness; but that experience did not change who you really are: still strong, still powerful, still in control, and still able to move toward healing. Deciding to move toward healing may be the only justice you ever get for what happened. You owe it to yourself, your partner, and your children to make sure that this trauma does not take you away from them any more than it already has.

Talk to a counselor. Sexual trauma is humiliating, but counselors deal with it everyday. It doesn't mean you have to take legal action or that everyone will find out. You are not alone. Don't let the one who took your power from you keep it. You deserve a lifetime of being sexually loved and enjoyed.

Voices

The Line of Sanity
Diary Excerpts from a Counselor in Iraq

Stateside (before deployment), April 20, 2007:

I have already seen the body-mind-soul disconnect. These soldiers are broken. There are some that suffer from the worst cases of PTSD. One soldier sees dead Iraqis constantly, and faces haunt his dreams. He gets "tunnel vision" and has choked his daughter, his wife has held a knife on him. He struggles with reality. Another soldier has extreme anxiety right before his disconnect. He explains it like someone else taking over. One soldier said going back to the field is like having the goddamn war all over again and seeing the pieces of his dead buddies.

A few of my concerns: Can these soldiers be fixed? Will I be just like them? Who will help me? I am scared of the unknown-but feel a peace knowing I am doing good for people.

Stateside, April 23, 2007

I had a soldier sobbing to me today. He was telling me about his "first kill"—an eleven-year-old Iraqi boy. He tells me he sees his face and all of the others he had to kill or be killed....I felt helpless and could only listen and hug him.

Iraq, November 2, 2007

Met the two mental health techs we will be replacing the other day and the new office. I wish that they did not go through the suffering they did to "hand it over", but they "paved the way" for better mental health care. All three of them needed counseling after it was said and done. The Doc (psychologist) said he will eventually get to practice again. At the end, he apparently was shitting and pissing in his room and not leaving at night to go to the latrines.

Iraq, December 7, 2007

Things are getting more stressful around here. I am not really stressed; it is the young medics that have never seen a bloody body or a woman's brains blown out like last night. Apparently, the woman's brain stem was still intact so it appeared she might live. The woman had a little girl who was five. She was covered in blood, and apparently has no parents now. See, it happens on both sides. "They lose, we lose." Human lives lost for what?

Iraq, February 6, 2008

Today I am no longer a "war virgin." Today, I did as soldiers do when they need to pick up pieces of flesh out of the rocks. What the hell? I can hear it now in e-mail—"How was your day?" "Fine, I picked up pieces of fucking human flesh in between rocks." I guess I held it together really well. Had to—needed to. I felt so badly for the company commander. Seeing his soldier like that. Looked as if the soldier were sleeping, but there was that look—even if you did not happen to see the buckets under him with blood dripping in them, his skin was gray. His vest covered in blood, I only remember the SGT rank, E5 gone, just like that, hoping he did not suffer—he was a blob from the neck down. It is hard to believe! Picking up pieces of someone who was just alive. Fucked up shit!

That sergeant is someone's son, brother, husband, friend—God, they will be going to the door soon, telling them. Smell is the worst. Could not eat anything that looked like meat. Blood, dripping from under the black bag… drip…drip….I took the company commander to see his soldier's face. The commander was in so much pain, I could feel it. My chest hurt and I was nauseated.

Why! Fucked up!
Me, picking flesh
Like it was garbage
Makes me mad!
I hate it!
Makes no sense!
Big piece of shrapnel with blood!
God why? Keep me sane, oh, Universe!

Iraq, February 10, 2008

Have noticed I don't like grease spots or wet spots in the rocks. It reminds me of the soldier and picking up his body parts. Kinda weird to me how I can freak out like that, I am feeling so much better. Those two days felt like eternal hell.…Sometimes I see why it is so hard for "my kind" (mental health officers) to exist and stay sane: *Sane—Insane.* I am on this line every day in Iraq.

—Mental health officer, U.S. military, Iraq[10]

What's Running Through My Mind Now...

7
The Questions

✦

Trevor sat down in the lunchroom with his colleagues. He'd been back at his civilian job for the last three months. Things were okay. Not great, but okay. It'd taken a while to get used to the routine, and some of the policies at his company had changed in the fifteen months he'd been deployed. He looked around. Men and women were chatting, laughing, talking about weekend plans. Their lives seemed carefree. Trevor felt a pang of envy. He wondered what they'd think if they knew the kind of things he thought about. Besides combat memories, there were the questions. So many questions.

When war takes you apart, you are left to put the pieces back together, to discard what no longer fits and to recreate, with the Universe's help, a new sense of wholeness. Questions begin the process, but when you're steeped in their depths, they can seem like they're all that exist.

Hold on and don't give up. There is another side to this and you will find your way to it.

As you search, keep this in mind: *no one can give you the answers.* You have to find and create your own answers to the questions running through you. You will eventually pick and choose, discover and accept new ideas, beliefs, and pieces that make sense *for you* and fit your new concept of what life and death mean.

Religion

If you were religious before war, you may or may not be afterward. Likewise, if you weren't religious, you may have discovered a new faith. War challenges every tenant of every faith. The stark contrasts of war's devastation, mindlessness, chaos, the randomness of death, (along with what it is like to create death), put most religions on shaky ground. Some people manage to hold on to their faith, and some people's faith is what gets them through. Other people feel betrayed by their faith, reject God, and everything they've ever believed.

Religion/spirituality is such a heavy topic and so key to so many of our most basic beliefs about life that I've devoted a separate chapter to it. But for now, understand that religious questions, anger at your God, feelings of betrayal, and rejecting faith are common reactions to war and its aftermath.

It's hard for families to grasp this, and you may find that your rejection of faith causes them to reject or pressure you. Remember, your family does not have your experience. They do not have the same questions you have. And there is no way for them to know what you know. Try to understand how your feelings about faith may feel uncomfortable to them and their perception of life.

Good and Evil

Closely tied to religion, our concept of good and evil is also thrown askew during war. We see good people do very bad things, and some bad people do, surprisingly, very good things. We also find that there are often no clear good versus bad guys in war. All sides have their truth. When you are living intimately with death and mutilation for prolonged periods, it's hard to see or believe in the existence and power of good. Your own experiences during the war will impact you most with this. In the enormity of the 'evil' done in war, losing faith in the existence of good is a common response. It takes time and a rebalance of being exposed to the 'good' in life outside a war zone to rediscover your faith in humanity.

Questions about good and evil also underlie how we interpret war, and the actions we and others take during war. Does evil exist on its own? Or is it the result of human intentions born out of fear, insecurity, and a desire for power? What causes people to commit atrocities? Are people 'evil' or are they merely human beings who fall prey to their environments and weaknesses? Where does morality come from? Are people basically good or are they inherently bad? These questions abound during and after war.

Meaning

What is the meaning of life if it can be taken so violently and at any moment? What's the point in existing if you can lose everything that matters without a moment's notice, without any rhyme or reason? What is the meaning of life if you can take it from another and not really feel anything while doing it? Why should you have survived when others didn't?

Why are we here? If the future does not actually exist (it's a concept in our minds based on expectation, but in time and physical reality it does not yet exist), then life becomes a matter of living in the here and now, because now is all there is. What does this mean for you? For your children? For the decisions you make about what kind of life after war you want to have? What is the point of life for you? What matters now?

Safety

The questions about security and safety are some of the most challenging. What is safe? What does it mean to feel secure? We imagine that we can shield ourselves and our loved ones from danger by our stealth, but is there really such a thing as security? What do you put your trust in? Your weapons? What keeps us from death?

When you know that the answer to that last question is *nothing*, it may seem that there is no solid ground underneath you anymore. And fear can become what you live by.

After war, nothing much is going to feel safe for a long, long time. Your concept of safety has been destroyed by gunfire, IEDs, mortars, landmines, lack of sleep, the possibility of sexual assault and many other situations that taught your cells to be on guard. It's been destroyed by never knowing who was safe and who wasn't, who to trust and who not to. The safety you feel now, is based on your ability to defend yourself, not what once would have been a natural trust in other human beings not to harm you. Your body has gone through actual physical/chemical changes that have altered how you react to your environment. It's going to take time to transition from feeling threatened because people were really trying to kill you, to recognizing that feeling threatened now is a conditioned response. It's hard to remove the actual threat from your mind. And harder to remove it from your body's learned responses.

You may perceive far more danger in civilian life than there actually is. And because you know how easily death comes, you may also be far more protective of your loved ones than they think is appropriate. It's hard to let go. It's hard to understand that you're not in control. Being protective gives the only sense of control that you know—because protecting and defending yourself and your loved ones on the battlefield was the only safety you knew. There was nothing else. Nothing was safe, and nothing much feels safe now.

Take a deep breath. No matter how hard you try to protect your loved ones, nothing will ever be enough. You are not in control of their destiny. And that's terrifying when you know just how easily and unexpectedly death comes.

You can't protect yourself from being devastated if you lose your loved ones. You may never fully trust life again. But the reality is that we have no control over fate's hand. It's going to take your body awhile to let the rational part of your mind help determine whether or not you are safe. What you know and what you feel will be two different things until the body has time to release the energy it has stored for protection and allow you to rest in the decisions your mind makes.

One thing you can start doing is questioning the beliefs behind your thoughts. Look at what thoughts make you feel unsafe. Ask yourself why you feel or think that way. Questioning thoughts can help us uncover our beliefs. And beliefs are what form our sense of reality.

I've found it helpful when fear or anxiety threatens to overcome me to take a deep breath and ask:

1. What am I thinking? I'm specific and write it down. I look at each thought, then ask one by one:
2. Why do I think this? What am I *believing* that makes me think this? Is it true? What would it mean to me if this weren't true?

It helps when I realize that many of my thoughts are based on things that I believed in the past; and at one point, those beliefs served and helped me to navigate life. My life and I have since changed, but I often find that in the process I simply carried old beliefs with me and never took the time to see if they still fit. So, the next question I ask is: Is this belief/thought still serving me? And if it's not, I choose to let go of that belief.

I'm not saying that this will work for all anxiety or fear—a professional counselor can help diagnose whether or not your anxiety or fear needs more medical care. I have found though, that for me, taking the time to question the beliefs behind my thoughts has really helped change how I see and experience life.

Purpose of War

Sooner or later, you are going to start wondering just what the real purpose of the war is and was. Everyone will have an opinion, but no one will have an answer. The war, for you, will be what you decide it will be. Your role and experiences will determine the meaning you assign to it.

You may find that you whole-heartedly believe that your presence was purposeful and resulted in positive results. You may also have deep doubts as to what was accomplished overall and whether or not your buddies died or were injured in vain.

There are no easy answers to any war—no matter how clear its mission or its enemy. War evolves as it transpires, and what may have been certain and solid at the beginning dissolves as new information and events unfold. That's why the longer war lasts, the less clear its mission becomes, because enemies are people who adapt, change, find new strategies, and new allies. New forces and new goals are established, and everything moves in a constant state of evolution. Who you were fighting in the beginning may not be who you are fighting in the end.

Let yourself ask questions, but do not invalidate your service or allegiance to your country because the answers do not come clearly. If you feel that you were used or misled or that your sacrifice is unrecognized, know that you join an ancient league of warriors who gave everything only to find that when they returned from battle, the winds of politics had changed, and with them, the whole purpose of the war.

War is a political tool. It rests on the decisions of those who decide to use it for particular goals they have in mind. In its best sense, war is purely reactionary—defending real property from actual, imminent danger. In its worst, it is the devastating consequence of the personal greed and ambition of a few.

Role in War

That said, how you feel about your role in the war will be related to your opinion of why the war happened and what its purpose was. Your war experience belongs only to you. You fulfilled a role that the military deemed necessary and useful. Whether you were on the front lines or not, every person attached to a mission knows that his or her role is part of the whole.

You alone can judge what you were asked to do in the war, and whether what you did or did not do correlates to your ethics. Many survivors feel a strong sense of shame for having done things that crossed their moral boundaries. This is a hard, hard question. Where does a soldier's personal moral code fit in to the gruesome, flesh-ripping, annihilate-them action of war? The fact that soldier's consciences throb with remorse is a reflection of their humanity. We go into war assuming that certain lines will never be crossed, that there are actions our troops will never take, that we're the good guys all the time, and that Americans are just different.

We're not that different. We uphold ideals. But ideals do not win wars. Death, and the destruction of property and economies win wars. Soldiers go into battle also believing that Americans are different. We don't torture people, we don't kill women and children, we don't laugh when a suicide bomber fumbles and can't blow himself up. No, of course not.

Of course we do. Our intentions may be altruistic—spreading democracy, bringing our brand of freedom, setting up systems that have worked well for us for two hundred years to countries that have existed for over three thousand. We believe we know best, know freedom, and we have the economic power to prove it. But what do *we* have to learn?

How you think about your war service will depend on where you see the United States fitting in with its neighbors, allies, and foes.

Some survivors feel shame, and some feel immense pride. Regardless of your role in the war, you were serving your country, and you have a right to be proud of that. When people suggest that your service was futile, remind them that if you hadn't been willing to go, their children would have. Every American owes you a debt of gratitude and admiration because without you, we wouldn't know what life without war is.

Priorities

There's nothing like war to straighten out your priorities, and fast. You come home with a sense that you're going to do things differently now. You're not going to take anything for granted. No more yelling at your kids, no more arguing with your partner, no more missing sunsets, and working like a dog. No, you know what matters now and it's not money, corporate ladders, football, or shopping.

Unfortunately, when you arrive home you're going to find that family structures and well-worn routines soon pull you towards returning to a life spent doing pretty much what you did before the war. Unless you make a conscious and public statement that things are going to be different.

Priorities can be life-changing. And they don't always come pain-free. What if, in the clarity of battle, you realize that you don't really love the woman you've been married to for the last twelve years? What if you realize that your law practice isn't what fulfills you and you find your mind pulling you toward moving to an inner city and working in public service? What if you find out that who you've been most of your life is not who you really are?

What then? War doesn't only take. It also gives clarity and the tenacious drive to do what matters in life. It's one of the few blessings of war.

So, what should you do?

Do what matters to you. Do what you know in your gut you are meant to do. Others may resist your desire to change as you remind them that they, too, could choose differently. Will others get hurt? Perhaps. But if you haven't been living authentically in the past, you really haven't been living in reality, have you? Your decision to take your purpose on this planet seriously and to do it before death finds you *is extremely important.* Listen to your instincts and make a decision to take action. Most likely you knew before the war what has now become all too clear. The war simply confirmed it. Decisions that realign you with your true purpose in life are usually ones that are long-lasting and take you to a calmer, engaging and more fulfilling place in life.

War has a way of making you fearless. When you have faced death and seen other cultures suffer and survive with the most basic of essentials for years on end, suddenly the things that most people are afraid of—the things that keep us small in life—no longer hold that power over you. You know that the only things that matter are people and that if you have your loved ones around you, you have everything. Now is the time to live boldly. To step up and really do those big things in life. You have a great advantage: you cannot be made afraid. After all, how can things like money or bankruptcy or having to start over ever be worthy of fear? Death is the only thing that can take anything away from you. So follow your heart and start living your dreams. You have the power to do it.

One word of caution: when you first find yourself without the adrenaline rush of combat, making drastic life changes can seem almost compulsive. You may crave risks, and you may not give a damn who gets hurt or what happens to you. Make sure you know that what you are deciding to do is what you are meant to do. You don't want to wake up in six months and realize that, after all, you really did love your wife of twelve years. You will know in your gut what you're doing is right by the quality of peace you feel. (That doesn't mean you won't be afraid or nervous, but that in your deepest heart you will sense a solid peace regarding your decision.) So, get clear with yourself before you take any major leaps. Once you know your intentions are right, be fearless in pursuing your dreams.

Responsibility

Many soldiers have an innate sense of responsibility. The more caring an individual you are, the greater responsibility you place on yourself for the well-being of others. It's important to remember that, as you transition from the structure of military life to life back home, you may find that you are over-responsible or you may avoid it. Part of what gets soldiers through war is the fact that most of what they have to do is decided by someone else. You can toss the blame off on the officer in charge—that makes what you have to do a bit easier.

But at home, you are usually at the top of the chain of command. You and your partner make decisions together, but you are responsible for your life, your health, your place in the world, and your healing.

You may be nervous about taking on responsibility, especially if you held responsibility during the war and lost people based on decisions you made. If you feel that you sent someone to their death, take a moment and look at the bigger picture. First of all, this is *war* we are talking about. Second, there are multiple factors at play during battle, including those we cannot understand. Did you really send someone to their death, or did they die while doing the job you gave them, based on the best information available, or the only decision you could've made at the time?

If you're relentlessly berating yourself with self-blame, remember that much of what we perceive to be our control is an illusion. We also confuse facts with intentions. Someone died, but did you want that person to die? Was it your intention that they die? Was there any way you could have done something differently? Really differently? If, in the end, you decide that you could have done something differently, you need to realize that what happened, happened. Let go of the bony grip of self-blame and realize that you did the best you could in that moment given everything that was going on. You were making decisions and mistakes while the enemy was also making decisions and mistakes.

We are human. We make mistakes. Fatal ones. Ones that send souls back to the spirit realm. We protect ourselves first when we believe we should've saved others. *We're only human.* We would all like to be god in war. Protecting those who should not die and killing only those who must. In the big picture though, human beings are at the very bottom of controlling how the earth's history plays out. Let yourself sink into the vastness of the Universe.

Finding Ground

The questions and the issues are going to swirl around in you until you close your eyes and try to shut them out, or come to a point where you realize there just aren't any answers that are going to make what happened okay. Much of our striving to make sense of war, death, life, and religion is an effort to hold on to a belief that these things can be explained, and if we could just get the answers our hearts would stop hurting and our guts would stop cramping up.

There are no answers. Not final, absolute, this-is-the-only-truth answers. What there are, are answers that will come to you, ones that will make sense *to you.* They may be something entirely new and spiritual or they may be traditional ones; but in the end, your spirit will find its own path and meaning for human life on earth. You can't grasp for answers. You will live with the questions for as long as it takes to find new meaning and grace.

Believe in the solid ground underneath you. It's there.

Voices

After War[11]

After war,
Flowers still grow
Thru cracks in sidewalks stained by blood

After war,
Survivors breathe
Thru lungs heavy with unshed tears

After war,
Houses wait
For ghosts to come home forever

After war,
Children play
In parks where landmines wait

After war,
Husbands hope
For a wife's raped memory to fade

After war,
Neighbors watch
For fear of saying hello

After war,
The dead ask
Questions the living cannot answer

After war,
Nothing remains
But fragments of sanity

After war,
Peace thunders
Thru silenced agony

After war,

Only hope
Is love a stranger offers

-a Sarajevan

What's Running Through My Mind Now...

8

Religion

✦

Eric grew up in a conservative family that instilled strong values and a sense of appreciation for the concepts America stands for. They flew their flag and went to church regularly. His grandfather had fought in Korea. At twenty, Eric enlisted and was deployed to Iraq. After seventeen months, he was hit by an IED, lost an arm, and suffered severe injuries to his chest and face. When he was released from the VA hospital, his grandfather, Jack, came to visit.

Jack had never been one to share his inner thoughts. His wife was the only one who knew he still suffered from nightmares and what she called 'episodes.' When he'd come home from war, no one had asked him how he was. Like most men of his generation, Jack kept the war inside and made the best effort he could to get on with life.

When Eric came home, Jack vowed he wouldn't let his grandson suffer in silence the way he had and, for the first time, he talked about the war.

"Don't tell your grandma, but I just couldn't believe in God after I got back," Jack said, sitting down next to Eric's bed. "How about you? You still believe?"

Eric stared at his bandaged stump and slowly shook his head.

"I don't know. I don't know what I believe anymore. It just doesn't make sense—all the time I was going out on patrols, I'd see guys get hit—I mean I can understand that—we're men killing each other. But the kids—" Eric's voice trailed off.

Jack nodded, then spoke in a near whisper.

"I was on reconnaissance, back behind enemy lines. I'd found a place to hide, had real good cover—no one could see me. I was on a hill and the whole valley was in front of me. There was a small village just below. It was around six or so in the evening when I heard the explosion—" Eric looked up when his grandfather didn't continue.

"Then I heard it. It was the most horrible screaming I'd ever heard. A child," Jack's voice trembled, he cleared his throat and stared at the floor. At last, he continued:

"She cried for hours. Getting weaker and weaker until—" A tear slipped down Jack's weathered cheek.

"I wanted so bad to kill those sons of bitches, but I couldn't! I couldn't! All I could do was sit there and listen. That's when I knew there's no God. At least, not any god I could believe in."

A God you can believe in.

Like so many who have been shaken by the unlimited cruelty human beings are capable of and the indiscriminate forces of nature and fate, war survivors face devastating questions about God and religion. After war, it's hard to find a god you can believe in.

Humanity is rooted in a rich heritage of religious beauty and bloodletting—our spirituality played out and supported by faiths that instill morality, uphold benevolence, teach kindness and acceptance, while holding their own as the true path to a Higher Power. You see the best and worst of religion in war. Every war is fought, in part, in the name of religion—either by believing that God is on your side or by the outright fervor to eradicate the world of people who believe differently than you. More people have died in the name of religion than have been saved by it. But it doesn't seem to matter. We continue to fight and we continue to bring God into it.

Whether or not you started out believing in God or practicing a faith before you went to war, you will no doubt have strong opinions or be confused about it afterward.

Most of our morality is rooted in religion. Whether or not you are conscious of faith, your viewpoint of the world, your beliefs about humanity's essential nature, your concept of what matters in life, and what happens after death are all based somewhere on religious teaching. Many people no longer recognize the particular faith attached to their world view, but you can be sure it is there. Most people have traditionally regarded the United States as a Christian nation—regardless of the large number of Muslim, Jewish and other-faith citizens. Most of our society's legal code harks back to teachings found in the Bible and much of it is anchored in the Old Testament. Christians, Muslims, and Jews revere these ancient texts as part of their religious heritage. The questions war raises are related to identity and even for the secular, religion plays an underlying and often prominent role. Here are some of the areas of faith that war may cause you to question:

Nature of Humanity

Our self-image is rooted in what we believe about the basic nature of the human spirit. Are we essentially good or inherently sinful? You may not have heard this discussed before, but the answer you give that question lays the foundation for the rest of your morality. It also is the foundation for how you relate to other human beings, your world, and to a Higher Power.

Those who believe that people are basically good often practice a form of spirituality that allows for mystery, common good, equality in worth, connection to nature, and the "flow" of the Universe's provision, abundance, and creativity.

People who believe that human beings are inherently sinful relate to a Higher Power that must in some form "save" them or be reconciled with to gain acceptance. Many traditional religions establish the Higher Power as an authoritative Being who must be appeased by confession of sin, good works, and/or other practices in order to be granted "salvation" from hell—also defined as eternal separation from God.

You may firmly believe one way or the other. Then in war you see unimaginable acts of good and bad. You see people striving to survive; good and bad actions become based on survival instincts. You see and experience vengeance, revenge, and rage so powerful that it kills and you kill. People who are supposed to be on the "good" side do things that are corrupt and so self-centered that thousands of innocent civilians and soldiers die and the good guys merely shrug their shoulders. Life doesn't matter to those it desperately should. Then you see people you believe to be evil commit incredible acts of compassion and display a softer side of their humanity. The lines of good and evil blur, and in the end, people become just people—not too much different than you, but not exactly the same either.

Your view of human nature will most likely change as you move through your healing process. Stay open to other possibilities and to the idea that regardless of beliefs, human beings are one species.

God is Love

The reality of war flies in the face of the concept that a Higher Power is loving and benevolent. Few can escape seeing children die or lose their parents, houses and neighborhoods blown to bits, and a whole society thrown into chaos without questioning where the Eternal Love is in all of that. Adults can often justify the actions of other adults, but rarely can we accept the death of children or those we believe or know to be innocent in a world of random violence. It gets even more complicated when we have directly contributed to that chaos.

Where is the love of God in war? This is a question that even the most learned scholars fail to answer. No religion can answer this. Whether you look toward a Higher Power or inward toward humanity, there is no love in war. There are loving actions by individuals who maintain a sense of grace and compassion in the most abominable circumstances, but there is no love on a whole scale side of things. The absence of this Love challenges religious ideals. We want to believe that the Higher Power we worship in life or by our sheer existence is loving. The major faiths teach this. War unteaches it. Life, after war, slowly re-teaches it in new way.

While families may feel that God's love has kept their loved one safe and allowed them to be reunited, the evidence of this love may be very elusive to the survivor. You simply cannot go through what a survivor goes through and not question this. You will find, however, that one experiences moments of pure grace on the battlefield. There is a Source of Life. Call it what you want. Too many miracles happen on and off the battlefield to deny it. When death comes within millimeters and still passes you by, or you die and your buddies bring you back to life, you can't help experience a sense of awe at the Great Mystery of all we human beings do not know.

Mercy & Forgiveness

Tied again to most faiths is the concept that the Higher Power is able to be merciful (not give us the punishment we deserve) and forgiving when we follow the prescribed tenants of our faith. Mercy implies that we deserve something worse than what we will get. This is tied to religions that believe human beings are inherently sinful and therefore alienated from the Holiness of the Higher Power. In order for people to be reunited in relationship with the Higher Power, human beings must somehow become "pure."

Each faith has its own assigned message for how people return to this relationship with the Higher Power. Those who follow a more holistic spiritual practice find that as each person is part of the whole, already good and acceptable in and of ourselves, the flow and movement of the Universe works through us for purposes beyond our knowing, and in ways that can not be defined. Instead of focusing on restoring a broken relationship marred by sin, concepts of allowing, awareness, and reconnecting to the whole are emphasized.

Mercy in our human life involves power. We must be in a position of power to grant mercy to someone we believe deserves something worse than what we are going to give them. Mercy is the withholding of revenge.

What is forgiveness? Forgiveness is our ability to accept the hurtful actions of others and set ourselves free from it. True forgiveness is an act of incredible grace—the ultimate act of accepting and allowing our ego to let go of our desire to lash out in anger and pain and create equal anger and pain. Forgiveness requires self-acceptance. It must come from a heart rooted deep in itself, where life is seen in a spiritual, eternal realm and the actions of earth are less important than the spiritual side of life.

I have trouble with the popular concept of forgiveness because it's been so ingrained in us that we *must* forgive, that people try to do it before they're ready—without the understanding that in order to forgive, you have to acknowledge and own the pain you've endured and caused. The forgive-and-forget concept of forgiveness can be a way of dismissing the real depth of your pain and keep you from acknowledging what happened. Some people think, too, that in order to forgive, the other person needs to feel sorry and ask for it. That's not so. You can't control someone else's actions or emotional response to you.

You really don't forgive someone *else* when you forgive, you make a decision to own your own power and let yourself go from the past. And when you set yourself free, you open up a new space for healing and wholeness to grow.

Why is it this Way?

War raises a lot of "why" questions. Why do people go to war? Why do we kill? Why do children suffer? Why are so many wars waged in the name of religion, when religion teaches us to love and seek peace? Why do we still believe war is a valid answer?

I can't answer any of these questions. And neither can most religions. What I can tell you is that the presence of the questions create an opportunity for reflection and give us the gift of being able to choose a better way. We want peace, we desire peace, but are we *being* peace? We want to live in a loving, compassionate world. Are we loving and showing compassion?

It all starts with tiny choices. With the little, tiny choices we have each day to either act out of fear or love. Religions aspire to lead people to a relationship with God. They aspire to bring out the best in people. They are an effort to embody the Great Mystery that life on earth is. But we already embody the Great Mystery—and regardless of whether we choose a path of religious faith or simply a spiritual path, we have the ability to create new answers and a new way.

The spiritual questions war raises will always be a part of the consequence of war. And perhaps, in a sense, they are the gift. The gift that allows us to dig deeper for answers, to figure out what we believe, and to realize that we are all spiritual beings on this planet who impact each other continuously. Questions that force us to grow as we no longer accept status quo answers and really take an inner look at our souls.

As your emotions percolate and settle, your spiritual questions and their impact on your life and world will rise and fall in cycles until, eventually, you find a path that is right for you. Do not feel ashamed for disbelieving. Questions are good. Open your mind and let the Universe guide you.

Voices

The Fear of Fate Striking

For years, I lived with a constant fear that fate was just waiting to strike and take Sasha and our son from me. I never—and I mean not once—said goodbye to them at the door without wondering if it was the last time I would see them, imagining that this would be my last memory of them. My chest would tighten up and I couldn't breathe freely until they were back with me, safe and together. Sometimes the relief I felt caught me crying uncontrollable tears after they'd gone to sleep for the night. I was just so scared that the joy and love and happiness we had found together was too good to be true and that, sooner or later, Fate would take it all away.

Life in post-war Bosnia taught me that there is no certainty. Life is very, very precious and if you blink, you miss it. It also stripped me of my faith in Christianity, which was a very hard transition for me because I had been very religious. I couldn't understand how God could be God and still allow people to suffer—innocent people, like mothers and children and teenage boys murdered to rot in mass graves. I also couldn't understand how people could be so vicious, so violent, so cruel, and suffer so much, then be expected by the international community to live together after war almost as if nothing had happened. The pain of the survivors I lived with and the stories we wrote each day for The Associated Press kept me face to face with the war—that, and the evidence of war damage in the bombed-out buildings and bullet-pocked apartments surrounding us.

As far as I was concerned, God had no problem swatting people down like flies. I quickly lost my sense of identity, and that left me out there with no ground to walk on. I loved Bosnia—still do—and Sarajevo spoke to my soul in ways I will never be able to explain, but the pain I soaked up in my heart was overwhelming.

I knew one thing: the life I had with Sasha and our son were the only version of "heaven" I was ever going to know. This was it, here and now. And because of that, every moment was precious, and every moment was truly lived. I didn't take any of it for granted. When my husband and I would begin to argue over something petty, I'd ask myself: if this is my last moment with him, would I want this to be our last memory? That prevented many stupid arguments and really kept our relationship focused on the positive.

But I was always afraid. I was always envisioning our "last moment"—and seeing in my mind how it would happen. When my husband would go out on some dangerous assignment—where there were rioting crowds or unrest, not to mention the danger of landmines and the possibility that someone could pull a gun and bullets would fly—I couldn't breathe. My world stopped when he was out there. What was worse was I was sure it wouldn't be from something expected; no, it would be something out of the blue. An accident when he was walking home from work; a stray bullet—there were so many possibilities that I don't even remember what they were. But my mind ran through all of them, in an endless array. The one thing I knew for sure was that if I lost my husband or son (as so many women around me had), my whole world would be over.

I lived in that constant state of waiting for Fate to strike even after we left AP and moved to the States. The reality of death and how fragile life is had been ingrained in me. I couldn't relax. Death was always near, and my heart was always half-broken anticipating what it would be to lose my entire world.

Then gradually, as time passed, healing began, and I started to rebuild my sense of what life and death meant. I began to believe that souls are eternal, and that life does go on; not with Jesus, but in a Universal state of wholeness, abundance, and beauty.

I felt like I was making real progress, starting to see life less through fear and more through hope until, one day, I had a mild health scare—an abnormal screening that later turned out to be normal. But this time the prospect of facing death didn't scare me, it made me incredibly angry. I realized that I had been living thinking that if only I'm grateful, if only I'm fully aware, if only I don't take anything for granted—Fate would somehow honor that and I'd be spared. The health scare made me realize that there is no protection. Absolutely no protection at all.

It threw me back into the pits of fear, but this time, anger compelled me to move forward. There was nothing—*nothing*—I could do. Not a damn thing. I could live my life fully aware, spiritually in-tune, in harmony with my life purpose and full of deep meaning, but, in the end, I could still be cut down in an instant. My husband and kids could still lose me or I them. The finality of realizing that there is absolutely no such thing as security, in the end, became very freeing. I stopped being afraid. I stopped holding onto life. When the old familiar tightness or "last moment" visions came, I stopped them. I chose not to live in fear.

And I still do. I choose not to live in fear.

-Britta Reque-Dragicevic[12]

What's Running Through My Mind Now…

9
Depression & Suicide

✦

Depression is a tricky thing; but even more tricky is what we think about it. We encourage depressed people to seek help, but forget that depressed people don't have the energy or motivation to pick up the phone and ask for help. Depression is made up of sadness, lack of energy, loss of interest in things that you formerly enjoyed, sleep disturbances, difficulty concentrating, agitation, decreased sex drive, unexplained crying, feeling worthless and guilty, and thoughts of suicide. These are also symptoms survivors may experience after war. Unless you suffered from depression before the war, what you are experiencing now may be from the war, from grieving, and the transition of coming home.

It's important to realize, though, that just because the war may be the root of what you are experiencing doesn't mean you shouldn't see a doctor and let her know about your symptoms. If your doctor diagnoses depression, she may prescribe medication that can help lift the symptoms enough so that you can address the root causes and stand up on the road to healing. Don't make the mistake of thinking that you should be able to handle these symptoms on your own. Remember, depression can have biochemical causes that only medication can treat.

Survivors aren't the only ones who get depressed during or after deployment. Families and spouses are also prone to depression as life changes and worry over a survivor continues.

Military life is tough. It isn't easy no matter how used to it you may be. It requires long-term sacrifice and giving at sustained levels that civilian families rarely are called to do. Not only is the lifestyle difficult, but the nature of the work exposes you to prolonged periods of worry, fear, tension, limited resources, anxiety, and life on the edge of death and loss. It would be normal if all soldiers and their loved ones experienced depression! Despite the conditions and environment that military families live with though, many military people tend to have strong views that depression or any emotional/mental/spiritual suffering is a sign of weakness. It's compounded by the fact that if you admit to any stress, your buddies lose trust in you. And many soldiers have suffered terribly during their service for having admitted to mental or emotional stress. However, depression isn't a sign of weakness. It's a sign that something is disturbing your body—be that chemical or emotional. Just the very nature of military service, conflict exposure, and the separation and relational issues involved lends itself to depression or depressed feelings.

A survivor typically comes home and experiences life after war in all its intensity and confusion. There is a constant pressure to feel less pain and more happiness than you probably do, and also a sense that if you don't "get over" the war quickly you'll be labeled weak or that there's something wrong with you. Despite the relief, homecoming can be incredibly stressful for survivors and their families and stress can play out as depression.

Many survivors aren't comfortable talking about depression—and many are not aware that what they are going through may be homecoming-induced depression. Families may be the first to notice the signs, but they too may get confused over what is normal post-war transition and what might be treatable with medication. Survivors and families also feel pressure that they should be extremely happy now since the survivor is alive and home. When depression hits, it may lead to feelings of shame and denial. Many survivors and their families try to hide depression.

You need to know that depression after war can be a normal reaction, and medication may help ease the symptoms. It's not necessary to try to figure out what's war-related and what's not. Talk to your medical provider. He or she can tell you what your options are and how to proceed with treatment. A counselor can also help you work through issues that may be leading to your physical/emotional symptoms.

Keep in mind that depressed survivors and their families often do not have the awareness, energy, or drive to seek treatment. Life after war is full of intense emotions, but it can also be experienced as non-experiences or numbness because the body and spirit is overloaded and simply cannot process anymore. If you think that you or your loved one may be depressed, then you need to talk to your medical provider. Don't let the stigma of depression keep you from getting help that might make all the difference in the lives of your children and your relationships. *Remember, there is always more at stake in your life than just you. We don't realize how profound an impact we have on our kids and loved ones. Getting help is an act of love for them.*

Depression Can Lead to Suicide

If left untreated, depression can lead to suicide. Depressed survivors and spouses, or family members who have lost someone in the war, may and often do consider suicide. If you are considering ending it all please tell someone *right now*. Put down this book and call 1-800-784-2433. This is the number for the National Suicide Hotline at http://www.suicidehotlines. com. Someone who knows what it feels like to no longer believe it's possible to endure the pain for one more moment is waiting 24/7 to listen and talk you through this moment. It's confidential, too. You can survive the forces trying to defeat you. Suicide is *not* your answer. It is not the only positive thing you can do. It is not your only choice. And no one in your life would be better off without you.

What people who haven't been through war do not know is that suicide—killing yourself—sometimes seems like the only answer to ending unbearable pain and unbearable memories. If you feel that way, or if you feel so guilty that you simply don't deserve to live anymore, consider this: your decision to let death take you now will cause intense pain and suffering—*more than what you are experiencing now*—in the people who need you most—your children, spouse, and parents. What will life be like for them without you? Without you whole? *Because there is a very real possibility that you can be whole again.* Sure, you may think that with your red-hot temper and how close you come to snapping and hurting them—that their lives would be better off without you. They wouldn't. *You are wounded.* You are not weak because you are wounded. And you're not crazy. If you die now, the enemy wins. You will be one more casualty lost to the war. You have come so far—surviving unthinkable trauma—do not let your life end now. I know you may not feel anything—and that can be the worst part. Not feeling. I know the isolation and being so misunderstood can seem intolerable, and the loneliness itself can be deafening. But you are a valuable human being and we need you here.

Just delay killing yourself for one more day. Just one more day or one more night. Tell someone you don't think you want to, or should, live anymore. As dark and empty and dirty as you may feel right now, ending it all isn't the answer. Why? Because it can get better.

There is hope for you and there is healing. And you can find wholeness again. Yes, it may seem impossible right now. You don't believe it. But *feelings are not facts*. It doesn't matter if you believe it or not—healing is possible and it can happen for you. No matter how fucked up you think you are. It doesn't matter. *Your soul is still alive and your body is still alive and if death had wanted to claim you it would have already.*

You can't imagine how good your life can be again. What if you had just hung on for another day? What if a year from now, your life is dramatically different—the pain a fading memory, the joy of your life back in your kids, lover—the traces of war manageable, you in control again. I'm not kidding you. *Healing is possible.*

Yes, you could end it all. You know how, and no one can really stop you if that is your final decision. But if you do, you will be taking life away from those who need you. And they *do* need you. You can't imagine or feel right now how much they really do need you. We do not know how very much we matter—or how the Universe plans to use us tomorrow to change a life and help someone else go on. *If you survived the war, you are alive for a purpose.* That purpose isn't to live in endless pits of pain and memories so horrific you can hardly shut your eyes at night. That purpose isn't to see dead people when you look at your kids, or to feel the sensation of guts on your hands when you're working. Your purpose is to experience healing. Your purpose will unfold to you in a process over time. And it is always meant to touch other lives in ways we cannot imagine. You have no idea how many good things in other people's lives may never happen if you are not here to fulfill your purpose in life.

Your purpose is real. You are the only one who can live your life and impact others in the positive way that your life was intended. Sure, you say, but right now nothing is positive about you. In fact, you're pretty sure you are causing more pain and harm than good. That's because you are wounded and your wounds need attention. Do not assume that just because you're acting like an angry, raging maniac that you are one. You're not. Your soul is simply trying to get you to pay attention and realize that coming home from war is not about coming home at all. It's about *living after war* and allowing yourself the time, space, and gentleness to do that.

A Taboo Subject

While in some countries suicide is considered an honorable action, in the United States, suicide is a taboo subject. We don't talk about it. Yet, as I write this, roughly one hundred twenty-five war survivors are killing themselves every week and the numbers are rising. For a war survivor who is struggling to keep the dark forces and the pain, guilt, and memories from completely overwhelming him or her, it may seem like a viable and positive option. You have to remember that survivors know death. They know how easy it is to die, and they know how to do it.

For family members, suicide may seem like a last resort, something foreign, something that takes a lot to get to the point of doing—but it is the easiest thing for someone who has killed and lived with death. It may seem like the only thing that will end the pain, the only answer, the last measure of control—and, for survivors experiencing intense guilt for what they did or didn't do during the war, it may seem that death is the only thing they deserve. The one positive thing they can do.

If a survivor is talking about killing herself, or making comments about not deserving to live—ask her how she plans to end it. You will not be putting the idea or the plan in her head. The concept of suicide can be so horrendous to family and loved ones that talking about it in a rational way, as if it were an actual possibility, seems wrong, impossible. *To someone considering suicide it is an actual possibility and many times the only one that seems like a rational answer.*

Talk about it. It is something real and it is really happening and you may be the only one who knows. If you feel that your survivor is close to killing herself or someone else—call 911. Call the Suicide Hotline. You *must* take action. The idea of suicide will not just go away. Once someone gets to the point of considering it as an option, *it is* an option and unless something is done to stop the process, it will happen.

Depression can lead to suicidal intentions. It works by causing *real feelings* of intense sadness, worthlessness, an inability to believe that you are loved, constant self-rejection, an inability to feel accepted, that others value you, or that you have any worth in the world. You cannot convince someone who is depressed to the point of suicide that he or she is loved. It's not a matter of talking rationally about how much that person means to you. It's not like in the movies. The person who doesn't believe life is worth living really *believes* that life is not worth living because that seems to be what everything in him is telling him. That's what everything feels like. You can't convince him out of that. Get help.

If you're a family member who has already lost a survivor to suicide, I want to tell you that your survivor loved you. War takes souls in ways we do not understand. It's not something to be ashamed of. And yes, suicide victims do go to heaven. It doesn't mean that your survivor was weaker than others or that he or she took the easy way out. Or that he or she didn't love you enough. You may feel intense anger and sadness for how your loved one survived the war only to leave you by taking his or her own life. I hope that this book will give you some insight into just how intense the emotions and experiences of war can be, and that you will find some comfort in knowing that your survivor was not in a position to make another choice *at that time*. The reality is that he or she may have died long before they ever came home.

Voices

Suicide

I found out one of my patients shot himself in the head (suicide). I got the message on my phone, it was 2058. This soldier was not even going back to Iraq. I think I am still in shock! Why? Nobody can tell me *why?* This young man was given the demons when he went to war! The demons fuckin' won! I tried so hard…he was smiling, only two to three weeks ago, telling me "Thank you, thank you, Ma'am, for advocating for me." Those words will fucking haunt me. I know they shouldn't, but they do. He did not deserve it, none of them do. Please, I just beg the demons to leave me alone, I don't know if they will, but I hope they will.

Why?…god, I spend a lot of time asking *why?* And people think I am fucking nuts? At least I care!

--

I went to my soldier's memorial. I thought: what a waste of a great soldier. For him, to be forced to make that choice. That chaplain does not understand more than the man in the moon. He had the demons—the pain that is unseen. I felt so bad for his wife and parents. Obviously, he had the monkey brain demons for a while. Why do people want to care after it is too late? All the "Brass" basically they are trying to "hold off Congressional," "Put a lid on it"… How fuckin' callus can you be?

--

I saw the news where the soldier hanged himself at one of the military hospitals. His parents simply asked if "he could be looked in on" as they had not heard from him since checking into the hospital. They found him after hanging for two days—why does it have to come to that? Why can't soldiers get help! They risked their lives for the U.S.—now they are broken, most without hope, lost, and full of guilt. I have not witnessed the hell until this place. Soldiers are suffering and all the system does is "slap a Band-Aid on!" I put him into inpatient care for what is supposed to be his own good? Is that really true? He loves the Army and would give anything—but would the Army do the same? No, of course not!

--

I witnessed one of the worse cases of suicide attempts by cutting I have ever seen. The wounds were so deep they had to staple them shut. The inner forearms were cut from elbow to wrist on both and it took everything I had not to freak out!

It is getting harder and harder and longer to recover on the weekends.

--

I met Mit...He is a Vietnam vet, 101st Fort Campbell. He was in A Shau Valley, the real one. If I close my eyes—his war becomes mine. He and I are officers, he asks the same questions –What about the soldiers? His pain, his sorrow, I see it in the eyes of my soldiers. When does it freaking end? Today I became angry! I know it, the same old feeling—angry at the Army, angry at the system, embarrassed of my leadership to send these innocent human beings to the wolves with the death sentence. From the pits of hell come calling all the falling...I cannot catch them all—exhausting—frustrating—one at a time. But I want to help more!

—Diary excerpts from a U.S. military mental health worker, stationed Stateside[13]

What's Running Through My Mind Now…

10

The Physically Wounded

✦

Losing a part of your body or function involves deep physical, spiritual, and emotional pain. The war is carried in your body and sometimes just looking at yourself in the mirror takes you right back to the trauma. There are days and nights of endless time, uncertainty, faith, fear, and, somewhere deep, a gritty unwillingness to give up and a probing curiosity that makes you ask: *why?*

Physical wounds may or may not heal. If you've lost arms or legs, hearing or sight, been paralyzed, or suffered from brain trauma—your body will never be the same again. That's a hard fact to accept.

In the midst of the physical changes, the pain, therapy, surgeries, rounds to physicians, the incredibly long waiting lists at the VA, physically wounded survivors deal with wounds to their self-image and their concept of who they are.

You may face questions such as:

- Who are you now that you don't have the same body you used to?
- Will your partner/family still love you?
- How can you have sex now?
- What are you worth if you can't contribute to life/family as

you once did?

- What's the purpose of living if someone else has to tend to your body?
- How can you be a burden to your loved ones for the rest of your life?
- How can you live with this level of pain?
- How will your family make it financially?
- What kind of parent can you be now?
- What's the point of your life?
- Who's going to be there for you?

None of it is easy. And none of it makes sense. You may be deeply grateful that you survived and wonder why you survived to live like this. The pain may seem unbearable and the sudden world of limitations overwhelming. It's the little things that bring out your anger, the sharp realization again and again that the road ahead is long and unknown. It's finding your spirit trapped in a body that can no longer do the things it once loved to do. And the struggle to know love in the midst of rejecting a body you never asked for.

But you did survive. There's a reason for it. No, you're not the same. As shattered as your body may be and as confused and wounded as your soul may be, in an inexplicable way there is a part of you that is still whole. Hang on to that part. You have survived. You are alive. The Universe breaths into you in a steady rhythm that pulls you into the next moment and the next and the next.

Your battle may be tortuous or simply annoying—your wounds may heal or remain, but in the end, it's what you *believe* about yourself that will re-create you.

So, who are you now? No, I mean, who are you *really*? Emotions will run rampant and wild, up and down, high and low—but underneath them lay thoughts and under those thoughts lay beliefs. It may take you awhile to accept the fact that you have physical changes that must be dealt with, but once you do, start at your thoughts and question your beliefs.

Who do you have to be in order to be loved? Why do you believe that? Is it valid? It is true? Who taught you that?

Who do you have to be in order to be worthy of your spouse, your children, your job? Are you loved for what you do or for who you are? If you're not loved for who you are, are you really loved? You are still *you*. And you deserve to be loved for who you are, not for what functions you may or may not have.

The cold truth is that for every survivor that has a loving support system of family and friends, there are those whose loved ones can't or won't deal with their wounds.

If your loved ones can't handle your injuries and you're facing their rejection, remember that you have the strength in you right at this very moment to survive this and get through. I can't answer why some people love deeply and some run, but I do know this: you are the only one who can validate who you are.

Whether someone loves you or not doesn't change the intrinsic value of your soul, your life, your heart. You may be rejected by those you love—and those you thought loved you—but while they are leaving there are men and women out there who are asking the Universe to let them meet someone who has your heart and spirit. Sooner or later, when your heart is ready, they will begin to appear in your life. Look around you. They may be there now, people who see who you are and have faith in the strength of your spirit. It's hard in the midst of heartache, loss, and tragedy to keep your mind open to the possibility that your life could actually someday be *better* than you've ever known it. But it's a real possibility, just the same. You may find deeper love, richer meaning, greater joy, than you ever believed possible.

Unfortunately, many people around you may think that it's the physical wounds and state of being "disabled" that's the hardest part to deal with; they don't see the silent side of being wounded. They don't see the mental battle, the spiritual battle, the battle to take a body you may not recognize and find a way to make it "you" again. They don't understand that there are a million losses in the loss of a limb. They don't get that the hardest battle isn't accepting what happened (though that's tough as hell), but it's in finding a way to believe that who you are *now* is valuable, purposeful, wanted, and *enough*.

If you're wounded or disabled, you need to know that you are in the process of creating a new identity, and that identity has to be built on you. Not on who you think you are supposed to be, or what you think other people expect you to be. You have to start at the core and feel your way through the darkness. Sometimes, oftentimes, one moment at a time.

Along the way, you're going to confront parts of you that you never knew existed; you're going to confront people who stare at you or stare away; you're going to meet deep compassion in enlightened souls and squeamish discomfort in others.

But just remember that they don't get to tell you who you are. That's your job. You get to decide who you are and who you are now going to be.

And who you are is someone who has a lot left to give.

Don't think so? Can't see that? Take a look around. You give to a loving parent just by existing, by their sheer joy in having you alive and with them. You give to children by showing them what matters in life, by listening, by noticing their world. You give to your friends by letting them give to you—opening their souls to deeper purpose in their own lives. You give to your fellow vets by understanding what they are going through. You give because you ARE. It's not a question of choice. You are part of the whole and interconnected to all souls. Your presence is enough. And if you are still alive, you still have love to give.

Don't forget that.

Voices

"They also serve who only stand and wait."

—John Milton

What's Running Through My Mind Now…

11

Control

✦

I first arrived in Sarajevo certain I could make a difference, confident that good wins out, and high on the thrill that comes from knowing that what you're doing in life matters. I had no idea how powerful war was or how powerless I would be.

In the three years I lived there, I didn't do any of the things I thought I'd do. Raise money for orphans and under-funded hospitals, create a visible, positive impact; publish a children's book that would help them deal with their pain—no. I became defeated, incredibly angry and a bitter cynic. Gone was the soft spirit I had arrived with. Gone was my ability to believe that anything really mattered.

Then I gave birth to a son. And he had a mother who was certain her heart was made of stone despite the tears that fell as she wrote. And that's when one thought changed my world:

I have a choice.

I could choose. Not the facts of the war, but my perspective. As I pondered this revelation, I could feel my soul crack open and a ray of light filter in. These words became a prayer that I clung to, day after day, my hope for the person I wanted to be:

I choose today to let go of the anger and the pain
I choose today to end the war and to live in the present
to recognize peace and let go of the past

I choose to have compassion for those who are alive
acceptance for those who are dead and
mercy for those who live with the guilt of what they've done

I choose to let go of my hatred toward those who have no conscience and
to forgive myself for my helplessness
in being powerless to intervene

I choose to celebrate life, to embrace the living, and to honor the will to
live in those who survived

I choose to remember that we are all living
by our deepest fears and that I, too, have felt
the necessity to murder, if only by killing the human spirit in another

I choose to be
full of life. To see beauty
to be alive and feel passion
I choose
wholeness

I choose to see beneath the surface and to celebrate what is
I choose to be
tranquil
and to be at peace
inside

The power of choice. How rarely we use it. How easy it is to fall into the
emotions and thoughts running through us and completely lose awareness of
the only power we ever truly have:

The power to choose our perspective.

I woke up to this and realized that while the war was real, its devastation
real, my wounds real—I had the ability to stop living like a victim, to refuse

to let helplessness and anger control me. *I had the power to let go.* I had the power to stop allowing the war to consume me.

This discovery changed my life, and set me on the road to healing. No, it wasn't easy. It wasn't a matter of positive thinking. I had to keep choosing, on a daily basis, to let go of the negative emotions, and let the positive in. To remind myself that I even *had* this power. But in the long run, this is what saved me. This set the stage and created space for healing. This gave me back control. It still took years to begin to feel whole again, but realizing I had the power to choose *how I responded* to the war gave me the strength to keep seeking healing.

What we experience after war is real. The emotional and spiritual wounds are real. Positive thinking alone won't change that. I don't believe the deep lacerations war inflicts can be cured by positive thinking. The power of choice I am talking about is not some magical form of healing. It is simply power available to each of us that we need to tap into. You can choose to think positively all you want and still be overcome with traumatic memories, thoughts, and feelings—especially if you have PTSD. You can't will yourself out of your wounds, anymore than you can will your body out of physical wounds. *Healing is a process that must happen by natural and supernatural forces over time.*

But by remembering that *right now* you do have the power to *choose* your perspective is the one thing that will set you further on the path toward wholeness. It will open your mind from its fixation on enduring the pain to crack open a tiny bit of freedom that will let healing get its foot in the door. Choosing to let go of the negative emotions gave me the platform to climb up out of the pit, see that there was indeed a blue sky above, and the hope that someday I could live above ground, in the warmth of the sun and sky. *It gave me a sense that wholeness was possible.* At the time, I wasn't sure if I believed wholeness *would* happen, but I was able to believe again that it *could.*

We forget our power and we give it away to thoughts that keep us feeling like we are victims, helpless, unable to change, and disconnected from our spiritual power. We have to take it back.

Much of our experience is perception. Events happen to us, by us, and through us, but it's our perception of them that creates our experience of reality. War sucks us into a vacuum of negative, death-related emotions and thoughts. Our minds react by protecting us with denial, re-shaping events through the stories we tell ourselves, and through focusing on surviving. We can get completely lost in the horror and become so engulfed in it that it blinds us to other realities—the reality that even as war is raging, beauty is surfacing, and the power of good is not diminished by evil, just overshadowed. Babies are still born, flowers still grow, people still love, acts of kindness take place, the earth continues to create and cultivate abundance.

Recognizing what we can and cannot control can be tricky. Deep emotions of self-blame, guilt, anger, fear, PTSD—all of them blind us. Even in situations were we perceive ourselves to be in control, we may not be. The Universe is always at work, pulling us in its continual flow of life, death, and existence. The only thing we can truly control is our perspective. In woundedness, the body and spirit may cause us to act out in ways we don't like or understand, ways that may even be harmful to ourselves or others. We may be disgusted with how we act, or by the hateful things that spew out of our mouths. We may wonder why we burst out laughing in morbid humor at the most horrific scenes (this is a common way soldiers break the tension in very serious situations—and often continues as a habit once they are home), or start crying over the stupidest stuff. For those with PTSD, the chemicals in your brain have been physically altered, which can cause a myriad of strange and uncontrollable reactions. There's growing concern that many Iraq vets have undiagnosed brain injuries from repeated blast exposures—and that, too, can cause unusual emotional and/or physical reactions. In our wounds, we may not be able to change our thinking on our own, until something comes along and blesses us with an acute insight that lets us understand ourselves better.

But when we can and do remember our power to choose, we begin the journey toward healing from a conscious place. We are aware and acknowledge that we play an *active role* in deciding what our future will be. We cannot control the past and often not even the present, but the future lies open, clean, and free before us like a tide-swept beach. It is full of possibility. It *is* possibility, for the future as an entity in itself does not exist. It is our *expectation* that time will continue to move forward that creates our concept of a future. That's why there is so much power in the realization that now is all we actually have. Because now *is* all we actually have. When you only have to deal with the present moment, as it is, right now, the monsters shrink down to tiny little creatures, your power suddenly becomes strong enough, and you realize that, yes, you can live in this moment—because *that's all you have to do.* Nothing has yet happened in the future. Sink into that and let it comfort you. Let the fear melt away. The future does not yet exist.

As your spirit begins to claim its right to make choices over how you think about things, realize that it is a process. Give yourself space to let your power fill you for awhile. Feel how it courses through your soul, giving you a sense of immense freedom as you grapple with aspects of letting go. We hold on tightly to pain and memories—because even in its discomfort, it gives context and meaning to what happened. We somehow hold on to those who have died by holding on to our sadness. Letting go of pain, anger, fear, revenge, and grief can seem like we are betraying someone. Letting go of guilt can also seem as if we are not taking responsibility for what happened.

We hold on and we hurt, and we hurt to hold on.

Choosing to let go has to be a conscious decision. It's scary because we aren't sure what will come after. You may not feel like doing it; but eventually, you will get to a point where it is do it or live in this hell forever.

Once you let go, what will happen is the pure oxygen of life will come rushing in, filling you, moving through you, easing into places that haven't seen the light of day in a very long time. The pressure of carrying trauma inside will be replaced with a sense of lightness, hope and possibility, a sense of breathing in fresh air and filling your lungs with it. You will be revitalized and reawakened.

Will you still be wounded? Yes. But wounds do not heal without air and sunshine. By letting go, you let the air and sunlight filter in and slowly, as your mind opens to itself, healing energy will move through. It takes a tremendous amount of spiritual and mental energy to carry non-life-giving emotions. Letting go of them will free you in ways that seem impossible just now.

As I let the negative energy flow back out into the vastness of the Universe, I knew that I had freed myself from a weight I was never meant to carry alone. All the negative emotions I had held so close inside had actually sprung from the fact that I cared deeply and intimately for others in pain. War had scraped across me leaving a bloody trail, but holding on to a state of woundedness did nothing to ease the pain of those around me.

We make the mistake of assuming that by holding pain (or guilt, self-blame, unforgivable regrets) we are somehow connecting with others or maintaining a connection. Let me say that again: *we make the mistake of assuming that by holding pain, guilt, self-blame, unforgivable regrets, we are somehow connecting with others or maintaining a connection.* Pain isolates. Only when we come from a process of moving towards wholeness can we connect with others and make a life-giving difference. The wounded cannot heal the wounded. The wounded who have found a path toward healing can share in the path of other's healing. You will not bring back your buddy who died by holding on to sadness and remorse. You will not change the future of an Iraqi family by continuing to mentally live in the war. You will not bring happiness back to your children's souls until you end the war in your own.

Choosing to let go of the pain sounds like a logical thing to do, but it won't feel logical to you. The pain and thoughts are often so intense they seem like the only thing possible for you just now. You may be very attached to your pain because of what it means to you.

I don't know which psychologist said this, but it impacted me:

"When the pain no longer has meaning, healing is instantaneous."

Think about it. Think about what your pain means to you.

Choosing to let go is a decision. It's a statement to the Universe that you are on a road to healing. That your life is not over because of what you have been through. That you are not going to give up and let death—in all its insidious forms—win. This is about letting go of what you cannot change to make space for a future full of possibility. About realizing that it's okay to be happy back home when your buddies are still getting shot at. You are not cheating them out of their happiness. You are breathing the fullness of life in their honor.

It's about making life-giving choices.

And that's what you have to do. Choose life. And anything that affirms life. Because you are still alive. And your life is not over.

Voices

How it Lingers

...A few days later, one of the medics was killed. He was my good friend, and I could hardly cope. It really tore me up. For some reason, a replacement wasn't sent out and I had to take care of the casualties of both B Company and C Company. I was wearing out quickly; the pressure of it all was draining me physically and emotionally. I got so weak I could hardly walk.

One afternoon C Company had to go out alone and I was so weak I just couldn't go. They were to be out only three to four hours, so they gave me permission to stay back at the temporary camp.

They all came back in tears.

The lieutenant had stepped on a landmine and was killed instantly. The guilt I felt was overwhelming. If only I had been there maybe he would still be alive. For over thirty years I've carried the guilt of that day. The guys didn't criticize me or blame me though. They told me that he had been so critically wounded that I probably couldn't have saved him anyway, but it was a sad day. I still feel the guilt and sorrow.

-Harry Kieninger, a combat medic who served in Vietnam[14]

What's Running Through My Mind Now...

12

The Enemy is Human

✦

At first Bill thought they were hallucinations. The visions of the dead. He saw them at the oddest moments, in the faces of people walking down the street, in children at his son's school playground, sitting in cars next to him waiting at the stop light. They'd haunted him for years—in fact, ever since he'd come back from Vietnam. His body trembled with fear when he saw the visions, even though the dead souls never seemed to take any kind of action against him. They were merely there, following him around.

Bill knew them almost by name.

But he never told anyone. He figured there was just something wrong with him and he was afraid that if he told his doctor they'd have him committed. Bill wasn't crazy, he just saw dead people.

The question was, did he really see them or was it just his mind?

Many Vietnam, Korean, and WWII vets will tell you that Bill really saw the dead. Because they've seen them, too. And some veterans from Iraq and Afghanistan will also be seeing the dead. If not in visions, then in nightmares, and in the gash knifed across their souls from the loss of human life.

Few people will talk about this, but the dead are real. And their souls are real, because we do not stop existing when we leave our human bodies. For those still living on earth, having the dead around them keeps them grounded in the past. It never lets them move forward into a future full of life and rediscovered meaning.

The souls of the dead want to be acknowledged and reassured that their lives mattered—and whether you actually feel/see the dead or simply can't stop thinking about them—the fact remains that they need you to let go of them in order to let go of you. It may be a matter of simply talking to them and acknowledging them. Sometimes it means going back to where they died and making peace with the land that has been desecrated and the cultures that have been permanently scarred.

What it always takes is acknowledging that the enemy is, was, and always has been, human.

The military dehumanizes those we are to kill in war because that is the only way to get caring, compassionate people to kill more than once. Enemies must become objects and not people. And so they do. But after war, they must become people again in order for us to heal.

The human spirit knows that the people faced in battle are people, not that different than us. But the mind and military conditioning refutes that concept. Still, in soul, soldiers know that the people they fight and kill are human beings. Soldiers may push it away and close down their hearts; and that is what costs them their souls.

Some soldiers never stop seeing the enemy as human. But for others, it isn't until you get off the battlefield that you begin to get the distance you need to do so. It can be both a painful revelation and also the key to redefining your soul. And it can take years to get to this point.

Once you do, however, get the distance needed to gain perspective, you can open yourself to thinking about those you have fought, killed, and defended more objectively. You realize that their ideals, values, and beliefs differ from yours, but they are at their most essential essence made of the same flesh, blood, and desires as you are. They are sons, daughters, brothers, sisters, wives, husbands, fathers, and mothers. They want to protect their way of life and their God. They want to rid their country of invaders and solve their own problems. They didn't ask for war to come to them, though some appear eager to fight for ideals that do not belong to the mothers and fathers who call the land their own.

Their politics are not yours, their ideals are different, and what they are willing to do to fight for their beliefs may be incomprehensible to you—but in the end, they are more like you than not. And when they die, a mother and father cry, a son or daughter burst into tears, and a lover's spirit is broken.

In death, politics matter very little to those left behind. We miss people, not their ideals. We miss the touch of hands and the taste of lips and the sound of laughter—not what organization or alliance they swore allegiance to. Strip off clothes, uniforms, patches, colors, scarves—you'll find that human bodies look the same. We are the same.

Except, we live as if we are not. We kill them; they kill us. We fight for democracy; they fight for power. We change their way of life; they resist ours. We believe we are right and *they do, too.*

Many veterans are returning from Iraq and Afghanistan not all that sure what they have fought for. Bush? Oil? Democracy? Terrorism? Human rights? There are no clear answers. Whether or not you know why you were killing insurgents doesn't make understanding the full impact of the war any easier. Most soldiers find some personal reason for going—and remaining—at war. You will need just as a compelling reason to get back from it. Part of this will involve re-framing how you think about the people you were fighting and the people who you were defending and giving your life's soulblood to free.

Simply stated, the enemy is human. People with nicknames and histories and favorite movies. People who liked to hang out with friends, who loved their families, who bought the latest cell phone, intended to make their lives matter, and wanted to have a future as much as you do. War came to them and they had the guts to resist it.

You need to see the war through the enemy's eyes in order to see the war in its wholeness. What was the war like for them?

Let's bring it closer to home—particularly for family and friends who know the enemy only by the words "insurgents" and "terrorists." Let's say one day you were heading back to your dorm from sociology class when a breaking news report comes on saying that a Muslim army has invaded Washington, DC. The army has been sent by a coalition led by oh, say, Saudi Arabia… to free Americans from the "evil" American President. Since the American President has been known to invade other countries at will and disregard international opinion, Americans need to be freed from this man who has killed nearly 4,000 of them seemingly for his own gain.

The Saudis are advancing in the city. You live in Washington, DC. The TV shows hundreds of Democrats rallying in the streets praising the Saudis for bringing an end to the American President's reign. But lots of Republicans are reportedly fleeing the city and others taking out their hunting rifles and getting ready to resist. You are shocked and really not sure what to think.

Then bombs start to fall and explosions rock your neighborhood. Your mom is killed. You grab your dad's handgun and vow to kill the bastards who killed your mom. The electricity goes down. How dare these Saudis think they know what is best for your country?! Sure, you didn't like the American President—but at least your mom was alive! Your friends join you and you start to fight the "invaders" every chance you get.

A guy in your chem class knows how to make bombs—so you get some and set up booby traps for the invaders. Your girlfriend thinks you're wrong. The Saudis are just doing what they believe is right for your country; after all, the American President has done so much evil to others. You argue with her and head out to kill the invading bastards. How dare Muslims tell a Christian country what to do!

You and your friends start to attend meetings where others like you form a resistance. The Saudi news now refers to you as 'insurgents.' Bombs go off and you wonder if your dad is all right. Your sister is on her way home from a school trip in Vermont. The Saudis want to stop her at a checkpoint and when the car she's in doesn't stop they fire into the vehicle killing her best friend, the driver. You are even more determined to rid your country of these invaders.

Months pass. You've killed a few of them, but mostly you're dealing with the lack of running water and figuring out how to cook without electricity. Coffee is sixty dollars a pound. Water is more precious than gold. You're eating stale bread that costs forty dollars a loaf. Your dad is deeply depressed and your little sister seems to be in a state of shock. You aren't sure where you're going to get enough food for tomorrow.

Every now and then you and your friends gather and make a run setting off bombs alongside key roads you know the Saudis frequent. Now, groups of Republicans and Democrats are also starting to fight each other—the Democrats support the invaders, the Republicans support the American President, who has been ousted and is reportedly hiding somewhere in the countryside. You don't support either of them. You just want life back as it was before the war. You'll do whatever it takes to help rid your country of the invaders.

Down the street, the Saudis have overtaken the adjacent suburb. You hear they're rebuilding a school that was bombed. They've set up a clinic. Your little sister is sick and the local clinic is run by Democrats. You hear they've been refusing to treat anyone who doesn't support the invaders. You don't know what to do, but you don't want your sister to die, so you take her to the Saudi clinic. Surprisingly, they're fairly nice. You don't really understand what they're saying, but they've got a translator. They give her antibiotics and send you home.

You still hate them for killing your mom and ruining your life. You still vow to resist. The invaders must die; it's the only way they'll leave your country. So you set off more bombs.

This is your life now.

Of course, this is a fictional tale, but it's not that far off from what life is like for many Iraqis. We are the invaders no matter how much we justify eradicating Saddam Hussein. You cannot disrupt the flow of human life in such a devastating way and expect that everyone will come out and embrace you. When they do, it is because they understand on a deeper spiritual level what you are attempting to do. That understanding does not make living through the war you've created any easier for them. And eventually, the sheer inconvenience, deprivation, and the constant state of terror from bombs, gunfights, and uncertainty will wear them down to the point where it doesn't matter anymore what good the Invaders came to do, they just want the war to end.

You may come from an experience of having Iraqis or Afghans hate and love you. You may feel close to the civilians who endured intense suffering and still found ways to show you how grateful they were for your presence. You are part of their society now, etched into their history, and the stories their grandchildren will hear. You have made a profound impact.

It may be hard for you to think about the civilians or the enemy. Or you may be unable to get them off your mind. They are a presence in your life and you have shared soul with them. When you give them back the respect in *your soul* that their souls deserve *as human beings* you will be able to begin to reframe your concept of what it means to continue your life as a human.

So, how do you re-humanize the enemy?

Begin by allowing yourself to see them as people. Forget politics. Forget religion. Forget whether or not they were al-Qaeda, foreign fighters, or simply teenagers caught up in gangs. You have to take off the cover of anger, vengeance, rage, and set it aside for awhile. What were the people you killed fighting for? What were they living for? What did life mean to them?

Honor their humanity by acknowledging that their lives mattered. Honor their families by acknowledging that your soul has become intimate with theirs in the act of taking their loved one.

For some survivors, the concept of 'making peace with the enemy' is too much to bear—too soon, too overwhelming. Don't force yourself. You're not going to get over the sight and sound of your best buddy dying. You don't have to let go of your rage just now. And you can't fake acceptance anyway. Just allow the concept to sit in your mind and let it be.

Eventually, as you move toward wholeness, you will lose the rage and find that your soul longs to make peace with those you have harmed and killed and with those who have harmed you.

You may even eventually return to Iraq or Afghanistan to honor the land and the people, just as many Vietnam vets have done—as terrifying as it can be for them—to find that the souls and memories that haunt them are, at last, laid to rest.

Others find that contributing to work that rebuilds war zones or supports the next generation of youth counters the devastation we have caused.

If you are a family member who has lost a loved one to the war, your healing will also involve seeing the enemy as human. It's hard not to hate those who took your loved one. And, unfortunately, in America, we are so insulated from other cultures that it is even harder for most of us to get inside a different culture and mindset and see how much human beings are truly alike. You may also eventually need to visit Iraq or Afghanistan—to see for yourself, to understand. You may also find healing through connecting with Iraqi or Afghani refugees and immigrants in the States. It's easy to hate a whole group just because one member hurt us—but when you have the opportunity to get to know someone from that group who is good, who loves their children and offers compassion to others—it helps to break down misconceptions and anger. You will learn that the war belongs to both of our cultures. And that the lines that divide us are sometimes the easiest lines to erase.

Whether you are a survivor or a family member, as you move through your journey toward a new definition of wholeness, you will move through the intense rage, hatred, and guilt to uncover a softer place where you are allowed to process the loss of human life in its deepest form. You will mourn and you will cry for the souls that have departed earth at your hand, and for the caring civilians you have left behind.

You may find that the souls of those you have met in war may never leave you. That your soul has so intimately touched theirs that they are now part of your existence. In this case, do not be afraid to speak to them—whether they are here or departed, whether you see them or not. Do not be afraid to accept them, not as enemies, but as souls who share a bond with you.

There is more grace out there for us than we think. The Universe reaches out with open arms, waiting to touch wounds with its healing life force, waiting to show us that our humanity is our greatest gift and our soul's most beautiful form.

Voices

Going Back

I recently returned to Viet Nam, after being there thirty-seven years ago. I journeyed with Ed Tick, author of *War and the Soul,* his wife, twelve others, four of whom were other Vietnam veterans. I am not the same person that I was before going.

I read *War and the Soul* in July 2007, and from that time on, my life took a direction all of its own. Something deep within me was touched. For years, I never even considered the thought of going back to a country that for me represented so much lost innocence, grief, terror, and confusion. There was a place tucked deep away in the folds of my heart that was dark and bitter. I have done a lot of therapy since being diagnosed with PTSD in 1996. I have worked very hard to somehow feel into and recover what I felt I had lost as a result of my experiences in Vietnam as a young man. I never even considered that the dark hole in my heart could or would, ever be so deeply transformed.

From the instant my soul said "Yes!" to going, the journey back started for me. My heart had been opened while reading Ed's book. Life took over and I followed. The money came, my friends and family were tremendously supportive, and on October 22nd, I stepped out of a plane and onto the ground, once again, of Vietnam. The journey for me, of past meeting present, began as I looked upon the Communist flag flying at the airport.

We visited many places as we traveled: schools, museums, Buddhist temples, peasant homes, cities, countryside, and old battlefields, to name just a few. Our journey throughout these places soon took on a mythical dimension, guided by an amazing grace and synchronicity that infused the journey with mystery and healing. At times, the others and I would just shake our heads in amazement at the divine grace unfolding. The seemingly small, insignificant moments were ripe and full of boundless mystery and healing. The script of the journey was being written by powers much greater than us. The Warrior's Journey home was very evidently underway.

As I moved along the sharp edge of past and present, that dark and bitter place in my heart was gently nudged, then slowly softened, and gradually opened. And what poured in was the forgiveness, peace, and beauty of the people and country of Vietnam. I heard words of understanding and even compassion from VC and NVA veterans. While praying in a Buddhist temple in Pleiku, I was grieving for brothers lost and those still suffering. I looked up and looked into the eyes of a fierce warrior statue, standing guard over the gentle nature of the Buddha. An arrow of understanding pierced my heart. In that moment, in the fierceness of those eyes, I understood that it takes fierceness in life to protect and preserve all that is good and just. My heart and soul were permeated with a deeper understanding of the true nature of the Warrior Spirit.

One evening, also in Pleiku, while sitting around a fire under the full moon in a Montagnard village, I was swept away into another world by the enchanting gong music and rhythmical, magical dancing of young maidens. Later, while walking down a trail with a few others, we looked up to witness the heavens and stars in a mystical alignment. There was the radiant beauty of the full moon, caressing her benevolent light on us all with soft blessings of peace and forgiveness. The constellation Orion appeared, yet somehow looking different from this side of the earth—with sword sheathed! And then Mars, the god of war appeared, nestled in the middle of the path we had just walked down and away from. I understood in that deeply magical and mystical moment that the entire Universe aligns itself and supports any soul's intention of peace and healing.

These and many other healing experiences touched the depths of my soul. Throughout the entire journey in Vietnam, the very palpable feeling of a country at peace, without the terror of war, touched the depths of my heart. That dark and painful place that had been tucked away for so long dissolved from the constant barrage of beauty and the friendly, welcoming eyes and smiling faces of the people, especially of the children. It was in those eyes and faces that I experienced the "welcome home" that I have for so long desired.

The grace of the journey continues. I am more at peace now than I have been in a very long time. I have a deep sense of purpose, and I now walk with renewed passion in my heart. The Warriors Journey home has only just begun and will not be complete until I bring all of my brothers home with me. I trust that the spirit and grace that I became aware of in Vietnam will continue to guide and support me. That dark place that was in my heart now is awakened and is a source of tenderness, strength, and peace. My heart beats with a fullness that reverberates in the depths of my soul. I am filled with gratitude.

—Michael Broas, Viet Nam service 1969-70, 4th Infantry Division[15]

(For more information on the Warrior's Journey, please see http://www. soldiersheart.net.)

What is Running Through My Mind Now…

13
Acceptance

✦

As we move toward a new definition of wholeness, acceptance is one of the most powerful actions we can take and give. Survivors need it from loved ones and communities in order to have the support that lets them look at the war and themselves and move toward self-acceptance. Released from the pressure to be what others expect them to be, survivors who are gifted with acceptance experience the safety needed to look inward. And inward is where the road to healing begins. Acceptance removes the "shoulds" from life and allows supported healing to take place naturally.

When directed inward and toward the war and enemy, your ability to accept your role in the war, what happened during the war, and what can and cannot be changed now, is key to redefining life and shaping the future.

We must embrace who we are *now* in the process. If we are constantly yearning for who we were before and focused on who we want to be in the future we miss the work of the present. And that work is to embrace our humanity in its deepest aspects right now, because that is where our deepest growth as human beings takes place.

We come from an either/or culture. But acceptance will open the mind to the reality that life—and humans—are full of dualities. What we must learn is that *it's okay to be who we are*. We can experience love *and* hate, fear *and* faith, joy *and* sadness, guilt *and* pride, anger *and* happiness—all at the same time. We can carry war and peace, wounds and healing. It's not a question of choosing one and denying the other. People just don't operate that way. We aren't either/or people. We are multi-faceted. We experience life as whole beings with a full range of thoughts and feelings, conflicting beliefs, and desires. It's part of what makes us so beautifully human.

Much of our conditioning to be either/or stems from religious backgrounds. Many religions teach us to embrace positive emotions and reject, or deny, negative ones. The effort involved in trying to do this leaves us, at best, judging ourselves; and, at worst, denying our true reactions to life. We are meant to experience and appreciate a full range of emotions. We are meant to know joy and disappointment, acceptance and jealousy, affection and indifference, satisfaction and longing. When we try to deny emotions that we are taught are not acceptable, polite, or "what good people are like"—we deny our own humanity.

It's only by acknowledging the existence of negative emotions, that we can choose to let go of them. If we try to deny that they exist, they persist.

If there is one thing war teaches us it is to appreciate and live in our humanity. When we dwell in our full essence, embracing the darkness and the light, we increase our ability to connect with all humans. We are all equal, and we are all capable of the most altruistic actions and the most defiling ones.

The rawness of life on the battlefront instantly reveals your humanity. You are taken to your most basic essence and forced to live from there. Much of it is pure survival. Only later, once you are back home, do you have the space to process what you went through. And, remember, it is a process.

You cannot force acceptance. You cannot take everything curdling through your veins and just decide to accept it. Acceptance is not just a decision—it is a state of being that comes through processing who you were, who you are now, and who you want to be. It comes from deciding to let go of your hold on the war, your pain, and anger. It comes as a natural result of the soul's growth toward greater consciousness. Don't feel that if you can't accept what happened that you are not healing. You are. Awareness is what brings you toward healing. We need others' acceptance of us and our woundedness in order to have the freedom to become aware and move toward acceptance of ourselves, our pasts, present, and future.

What do we have to accept?

We have to accept that we will never be who we were before. We have to accept that who we are right now is okay. The changes we go through, the pieces of us that were cut away and are now filling in with new tissue or are gone forever—have to be accepted. We are literally being re-created—physically as time and rest bring renewed cells and energy; mentally as we open to new perspectives and worldviews; spiritually as we shed old beliefs and take on new.

As we learn to let go and take control of our perspective, we take power away from war and death and allow life to infuse us with new meaning. This happens slowly. You cannot come back from war and expect to be healed in a matter of weeks.

There are aspects of war that will never leave you. There are wounds that will always be tender no matter how whole you become. The war will never be far away. But you will learn to be whole in spite of it—a new sense of whole. You will integrate war into your life, because it is now a part of you. You will be re-born as someone who has lived through death, survived, and come back to experience the fullness of life after war.

I know this may all sound impossible just now. When you're hurting and reliving horror and nightmares and can't get the smell of burning flesh out of your senses, the thought that someday you might be whole again is hard to believe. You don't have to believe. The Universe will believe for you. Let those who have come before and found a new sense of wholeness stand in the gap for you. We believe in you. And remember, this is a journey—a process—not an event. *It's okay to be who are you are right now.*

Families also move toward acceptance in their own lives as they experience changes in a survivor. It can be easy to overlook your own pain, loss, grief, and exhaustion when faced with the enormity of a survivor's pain. But you also need the support of acceptance. And for you, the strongest form you can get is self-acceptance. Let go of thinking you need to change, that you are responsible for healing, that you must be someone stronger than you believe you are right now.

It's okay to be who you are right now, too. You also have wounds from separation, worry, fear, overload, and the stress of feeling responsible for making sure your relationship doesn't fail. Let go of the illusion of control. The only thing you can control is your perspective. Through your perspective you can *influence* your children and other family members—but you cannot control their response to the survivor, or their level of commitment.

No matter how hard you try or how supportive you are, there are times when the relationship will not survive. It's another high cost of war. The reality is that not every marriage or relationship will survive the changes of life after war. Every person is different, and every relationship has its own strengths and weaknesses. If you know in your soul that the relationship has not survived or cannot survive, this is a place for you to embrace acceptance as well. This is a wound that will need time to heal. It can be devastating to all involved—and compounds the losses caused by war. But it does happen, and you are not the only one it will happen to.

Military relationships have inherent risks and threats to them. War only exacerbates that. Some relationships were ending long before war came along. For others, war brings out obstacles that just can't be overcome. For survivors who suffer from extreme symptoms of PTSD, the violence and fear it invokes may be enough to end a relationship immediately. (If you feel in danger or threatened, you should take immediate action to move to a place of safety. A survivor with intense PTSD *cannot* focus on healing a relationship from his or her state of woundedness.)

If you are a survivor who has come home to find that your partner is no longer in love with you, you face an especially hurtful homecoming. The sense of isolation and loss of support can be devastating—even more so if you counted on that support during your deployment. As hard as it is, you will survive this. It's no comfort in the midst of heartbreak, I know, but sometimes the Universe takes a relationship from us in order to move us toward a life that is more aligned with our purpose and the person we are becoming. Grieve your loss. Move inward and allow yourself space to focus on healing now.

As we sift through the shattered remains of our identities and the pieces of our lives strewn about after war, we must find meaning in our changed selves and make it part of our new identity. Much of who we were will be left behind. Some parts of us will be picked up and refashioned. Other parts will come to us new, from unexpected places, and unexpected blessings.

The Universe moves in a continual flow of abundance, creativity, life, death, and re-creation. You are part of that flow. Acceptance is a gift that brings meaning to your new life, and reverence to your old.

Voices

Letting Go[16]

We hold on to the past. And when we refuse to let go, the Universe will come and take it away. A job, a relationship, a plan, a priority. If we are not moving forward toward consciousness, we will be moved forward. The Universe does this, not to be cruel, but to set us free, to move us closer to that which will truly fulfill us.

—Unknown

What's Running Through My Mind Now...

14
Honor

✦

Diego fastened the last button on his dress uniform. A row of medals lined his chest. He'd served proudly and believed his role in Afghanistan had been honorable. At 34, he was the youngest member of the local American Legion. The town was holding a parade in honor of its vets and Diego would be raising the flag for the start of the ceremony. He felt a wave of pride sweep over him as the crowd sang the Star Spangled Banner. People clapped and cheered once the flag reached full staff.

That afternoon, he sat at the Legion bar and ordered a cold beer. An older gentleman eased into the stool next to him and asked for a whiskey. Diego nodded as the man glanced at the medals on Diego's coat.

"You seen action, huh?" the older man said, taking a sip.

"Afghanistan." Diego judged the man to be somewhere near sixty.

"Those pins don't mean much, do they?" the older man said.

"Sir?" Diego could feel the heat rise.

"Vietnam. Three years. I've got a box of medals stashed away in some drawer. They never brought me any honor. I had to hang my head in shame when I came home."

Diego wasn't sure what to say. He took a swig of beer and drained the frosted glass, when the old warrior spoke again.

"There's honor in war, boy. Just isn't any at home."

Diego carried the man's words around for days. He wondered what life had been like for the older vet. He wondered, too, at the pins on his own chest. He'd earned them, but he had to admit, the small pieces of medal and ribbon didn't give much comfort when the nightmares of combat invaded each night. Still, they meant something, didn't they? Proof that he'd served well. Evidence of service the VA would request twenty years from now when he would apply for disability for a wound he'd taken in his leg.

Honor. What is it? And what does it mean? It's a rather elusive concept associated with war; defined by high esteem for having displayed high standards of behavior. It's a form of respect so great that we change how we act toward a person we honor.

We honor someone by acknowledging that what they have done and endured took incredible strength and resilience. We honor someone when we value the meaning of their actions. We honor someone when we treat their wounds and scars and post-war life as real and relevant and meaningful. And we honor survivors by accepting that what they have given and lost and sacrificed means something to us.

Veterans are generally good at honoring each other. They find many ways to express honor for buddies lost in battle and memories that only the people in their platoon know—the efforts, strengths, suffering, and courage that only they witnessed in each other. Some veterans keep websites dedicated to their unit; others hold annual reunions; some write books. One Iraq veteran I know created a memorial to fallen friends by buying a headstone, having his buddies' names engraved on it, then placing a flagpole and planting flowers around the site. This is at a resort he owns, and vacationers are allowed to honor the fallen soldiers while he is able to share what honor and service mean to him.

It's necessary for you to honor others, but as a survivor, you must also honor yourself as a soul who recognizes your place in the Universe and among humanity. You must honor your experience and your pain, for when you do, you create meaning around it, giving it definition and place. And you must honor your experience to teach the rest of us how to honor you.

It's easier said than done. And yet, if we do not value ourselves as human beings, we fail to give our lives the meaning they're meant to have. Your spirit deserves to be honored for its sheer ability to survive. Your body deserves the honor of recognizing the need for rest and renewal. Your heart needs to be honored for holding on to a thread of compassion in a world of violence. And your pain must be honored for it to be healed.

Part of making peace inside is honoring your fragility and your resilience. It's hard to step back and detach enough to think of yourself a bit more objectively, but when you do, you gain a profound respect for what human beings are capable of surviving and protecting. You experience the fullness of your humanity, and come to understand that when you honor yourself for what you have survived, you develop purpose in your life. You make peace inside when you stop berating yourself for not living up to false expectations and start accepting that, as a human being, there is room for grace. When you honor your humanity, you honor others' humanity. Understanding takes root and peace is grafted in.

You honor yourself when:

- You don't deny that you are in pain.
- You let others give back to you.
- You speak up about the war and what it was like.
- You take the time to rest.
- You take your medications.
- You take care of your body by eating well and not abusing drugs or alcohol.
- You give others a chance to understand what is happening with you—instead of assuming they should know.
- You take responsibility for your own healing journey.
- You recognize that your life has a profound impact on those around you.

And as you honor yourself, you will find that your own role as a warrior will be more meaningful and respected. You are a warrior. It is part of your identity. As you move through depths of emotions and currents that take you from abject horror to glimpses of wholeness and back again, you will go through changes in how you think of yourself as a warrior. Pride, anger, shame, self-blame, humiliation, uncertainty, honor, respect—these may ripple through you as you move toward healing. Ultimately, you will honor the depths of courage you have known, the soul-numbing fear, the taste of death and the exhilaration of life—it will become a part of you that anchors you to your life.

Separated from war, you grow into a sense of your place in the Universe. As you listen to your gut instincts (not your conditioned survival reactions, but your intuitive responses), you begin to move toward a place that is aligned with your purpose in life. You cannot see this in the blindness of pain. The immediacy of pain shuts it out. But as you move toward healing, even the pain will take on meaning as you find that the Universe has a purpose for you.

Human life is a never-ending web of souls touching other souls. It's how the Spirit moves through earth—we do not see all the implications and reverberations of our lives, but they happen nonetheless. We act, and ripples of actions extend out for generations. This awareness sends a knife blading through us when we realize the long-lasting impact of war. But it should also bring comfort. Because even in war, new life is formed and positive things happen afterward that we cannot imagine. Our actions have known and unknown implications for generations of lives. When we honor our place in this world we honor the impact we have on the Universe.

And honor brings peace.

Voices

"The deepest honor we can give is to celebrate life with every choice we make."

—Anonymous[17]

What's Running Through My Mind Now…

15

Beauty from Ashes

✦

You're stuck in the memories, the questions, the sense of futility of life after war. You're angry, sick about things you've seen and done, and pretty certain that no one in the world gives a damn. Life has little purpose—if any. Death has no rationale, rhyme, or reason. God is—well, if there is a god, he's a fucking liar. You know your bitterness is causing you to withdraw from your spouse, but you're not about to share the putrid thoughts running through your mind. Your kids are a bit afraid of you—all right, they're avoiding you. And it cuts you to the bone when you see pain flash across their eyes when you yell at them. You don't mean to yell at them. But you're just so—tense. You don't know what to do. Your unit has been through demobilization, you've been informed about PTSD—only eighteen percent of you are going to get it and well, you don't have it. You thought life back home would be easier than this. But this is so much worse than anything you imagined.

And so you've read this book.

It's interesting, you think, filled with a lot of stuff you're not quite sure you get, but you still feel the exact same way as when you began reading it. The nightmares are still keeping you from sleep, the war still feels more real than this life at home and the thought of "creating sacred space" and "humanizing the enemy" are so far from what you're ready to do that all you can do is laugh.

That's okay. This book isn't a quick fix. There is no quick fix. This book is meant as a guide—as something to turn to when you want to put what you're going through into words and you don't know how. This book is for you.

What it is, is a beginning. A place to start. And from here, with your willingness, you begin a journey toward rediscovering and redefining your life. You begin a time of exploration—although much of it will be unconscious and little of it can be discovered by actually looking. You are in a place now where all you can do is exist—be still and be. You don't know who you are and that's okay.

You are being re-born. You will recognize remnants of your old self and not others. You are rebuilding your soul. And this takes time, patience, self-compassion, and a tiny, tiny seed of faith. Not much, a mustard-seed size is enough, if you want to move mountains.

Here's a secret: you hold on to that tiny seed of faith, and the mountains will move themselves.

The fact that you've read this book means you've held on. You believe there is hope. You want healing and you have not given up.

Don't give up. Don't *ever* give up. That's what my father said during his ten-month battle with cancer. *As long as there is hope, you never give up.* He took that hope and that faith with him to the other side, and I'm pretty sure he's with my medic sister, Sgt. Molly Reque, now as she rescues wounded soldiers somewhere north of Baghdad.

There is hope for you.

There is a life of wholeness out there. There is meaning to what you have become.

And there is healing.

Not erasure. But healing. Eventually, as you open to a new sense of wholeness, the pain will ease, the nightmares will fade, the things you can't accept today will become a part of your soul. Not today. Maybe not tomorrow.

But it will happen. Quietly. One moment at a time. As the tears fall. As you remember. As you feel your soul holding you in its tender embrace. As the waves of horror wash over you anew, and the numbness disappears.

It will happen.

And we will be here to catch you when you fall.

For your soul is still beautiful.

And you are so very, very loved.

What's Running Through My Mind Now...

RESOURCES

www.lifeafterwar.org Web site for this book and support resources for veterans, families, healthcare practitioners, and communities aimed at healing and finding renewed meaning in life after war.

www.Soldiersheart.net Soldier's Heart is a veterans' return and healing project addressing the emotional and spiritual needs of veterans, their families, and communities. Soldier's Heart promotes and guides community-based efforts to heal the effects of war based on strategies presented in Dr. Ed Tick's book, *War and the Soul.*

www.healingcombattrauma.com Resources for and about healing combat trauma. The focus is on effective therapeutic care — medical, psychological and legal — plus analysis and context — and the slant is apolitical.

www.ncptsd.va.gov National Center for Post Traumatic Stress Disorder

www.rainn.org National Sexual Assault Hotline 1-800-656-4673

www.suicidehotlines.com National Suicide Hotline 1-800-784-2433 Available 24/7.

VA Suicide Hotline, 1-800-273-8255, then press 1. Available 24/7.

www.welcomehomesoldier.com Writing seminar and ongoing weblog from Remy Benoit, historian, author, editor, and educator for Veterans and others who believe in learning from and writing their own history.

www.shamanism.org The Foundation for Shamanic Studies, a source for information and products relating to the study of shamanism and shamanic healing.

www.iava.org Founded in June 2004, *Iraq and Afghanistan Veterans of America* is the nation's first and largest group dedicated to the troops and veterans of the wars in Iraq and Afghanistan, and the civilian supporters of those troops and veterans.

www.fallenherosfund.org The Intrepid Fallen Heroes Fund is a leader in supporting the men and women of the Armed Forces and their families.

Begun in 2000 under the auspices of the Intrepid Museum Foundation, and established as an independent not-for-profit organization in 2003, the Fund has provided close to $60 million in support for the families of military personnel lost in service to our nation, and for severely wounded military personnel and veterans.

www.woundedwarriorproject.org   The mission of the Wounded Warrior Project is to honor and empower wounded warriors. To raise awareness and enlist the public's aid for the needs of severely injured service men and women. To help severely injured service members aid and assist each other. To provide unique, direct programs and services to meet their needs.

www.jamesray.com Create Harmonic Wealth in all areas of your life with James Arthur Ray: financially, relationally, mentally, physically, and spiritually.

NOTES

1 Cory, John. *Blues for Armageddon.* 2008. http://www.john-cory.com/images/Blues_for_Armageddon_Book.pdf.

2 Ibid.

3 "Iraqi Orphanage Nightmare," *CBSNews.com*, 18 June 2007, http://www.cbsnews.com/stories/2007/06/18/eveningnews/main2946007.shtml.

4 Story, Lonnie D. "Before I Was Born." 2007.

5 "Most Often Asked Questions Concerning Homeless Veterans," National Coalition for Homeless Veterans, http://www.nchv.org/background.cfm.

6 Benoit, Remy. *warm, glowing woman.* 2008.

7 Kubler-Ross, Elizabeth. *On Death and Dying.* New York: Scribner, 1969.

8 Cory, John. *Blues for Armageddon.*

9 "Fact Sheet: Military Sexual Trauma," National Center for PTSD, http://www.ncptsd.va.gov/ncmain/ncdocs/fact_shts/military_sexual_trauma_general.html?opm=1&rr=rr1758&srt=d&echorr=true.

10 Anonymous. "Line of Sanity: Diary Entries from a Counselor in Iraq." 2008.

11 Reque-Dragicevic, Britta. "After War." 2003.

12 Reque-Dragicevic, Britta. "The Fear of Fate Striking." 2008.

13 Anonymous. "Suicide." 2008.

14 Keininger, Harry. *When Can We Come Home? Understanding the Vietnam Veteran.* Indianapolis: A-1, 1998.

15 Broas, Michael. "Going Back." 2008.

16 Unknown. "Letting Go." 2008.

17 Anonymous. Quote. 2008.

LaVergne, TN USA
08 January 2010
169408LV00002B/21/P